Contents

LIVING WITH A HYPERACTIVE CHILD

By the same author

MUSIC FOR MENTALLY HANDICAPPED PEOPLE

HUMAN HORIZONS SERIES

LIVING WITH A HYPERACTIVE CHILD

by

MIRIAM WOOD

With a Foreword by Vicky Rippere,
MA, PhD, BSc, MPhil

Illustrated by Janne Marie Bunker

A CONDOR BOOK
SOUVENIR PRESS (E & A) LTD

ISBN 0 285 64986 8 casebound
ISBN 0 285 64987 6 paperback

Printed in Great Britain by
Photobooks (Bristol) Ltd

Dedicated to my family, Leslie, Tanya and John and to the restoration of tranquillity in the home.

Foreword

Parents of hyperactive children face many problems. First there are the problems which arise from coping with a child who may behave like a tornado at home, outlive his welcome elsewhere, require constant supervision by day and hardly sleep at night. And second, there are the problems which arise from trying to find appropriate help with such a child in the absence of relevant public facilities.

In Britain at the present time, hyperactivity is not a recognised category of childhood disorder with appropriate statutory provisions. Indeed, the Establishment still seems preoccupied with the question of whether hyperactivity should be considered to exist as a syndrome and, if so, what is its prevalence. It may well be that hyperactivity is not a syndrome in the sense that cretinism or mongolism are syndromes, packages of characteristic signs and symptoms with an objectively definable aetiology and typical prognosis. But, in the present state of knowledge, neither are most psychiatric conditions which are recognised and provided for. Whether hyperactivity is or is not a syndrome is, in any case, largely irrelevant to the parents of hyperactive children, since, syndrome or not, they are left holding the baby. Whether families of hyperactive children receive help that is actually helpful from their general practitioners, health visitors, paediatricians, child psychiatrists, educational and clinical psycologists and teachers often seems to be a matter of chance. As many of Mrs Wood's informants describe, the 'solution' proposed – reassurance that the child is 'normal' and will 'grow out of it' and, if this stratagem is unsuccessful, Valium for the mother, whose anxiety is regarded as the cause of the child's problem rather than as an understandable effect – may be quite irrelevant, misguided, and impertinent.

Despite the shortcomings in provisions for hyperactive children, some fortunate, or perhaps persistent, families do manage to obtain positive help through official channels, but so many do not that in the past six years a vigorous self-help movement has developed under the aegis of the Hyperactive Children's Support Group. Founded in 1977, HACSG now has over a hundred branches all over Britain and a membership in the thousands, indicating the existence of a vast need in the community which statutory provisions do little to meet or even acknowledge. The Group's efforts to obtain much-needed funding from the Department of Health and Social Security read like a chapter of *Catch 22*. Public funds cannot, it seems, be allocated for support of the Group – but at the same time government funded advisory services refer parents of hyperactive children to the Group. Meanwhile, its founders are perpetually on the verge of being buried alive in tons of letters from desperate mothers seeking help and advice on how to cope with their miserable, intractable, self-winding children, advice which they have been unable to obtain elsewhere, since their supposedly deviant children are, of course, 'normal and will grow out of it'.

What is needed to break this unhappy stalemate is greater public awareness of what it means to live with a hyperactive child. Mrs Wood's book addresses itself both to parents of hyperactive children and to people who do not know what it is like to live with a hyperactive child. She notes that before she discovered HACSG, she had no contact with other parents sharing similar problems and as a result of her isolation she felt lonely and frustrated. People in a similar position are likely to find it beneficial to read of the experiences of other families and of the solutions they have found to some of their everyday difficulties. And if others who do not share these problems also learn more about them, their increased knowledge and understanding may also help these parents, who so often meet with misunderstanding and censure for their child's apparent 'brattiness' – the more so if these others work professionally with children. Moreover, greater public understanding and awareness of the unmet needs of families of hyperactive children may make it more difficult for the government to maintain its present ostrichlike posture in relation to these needs.

It emerges clearly from Part Three of Mrs Wood's book that the 'experts' in child psychology and psychiatry are divided on the matter of hyperactivity. It is also clear that their failure to reach agreement about whether the condition exists and what to do about it contributes to maintaining the status quo in relation to public provisions for these children's needs. The time has come when it is necessary to look to other experts for guidance out of the impasse. The real experts on the problems of living with hyperactive children are these children's parents and families. It is time for their expertise to be acknowledged, and Mrs Wood is to be congratulated on her efforts to bring it to public attention.

Vicky Rippere
August, 1983

Acknowledgements

The author would like to thank everyone who has aided in the preparation of this book.

Thanks to the parents of hyperactive or allergic children who responded so wonderfully when asked to share their experiences in the upbringing of their children. Thank you also to the unnamed doctors who acknowledged my enquiries and took time to share their views.

In particular, thanks are expressed to the following persons: Sally Bunday and Vicky Colquhoun of the Hyperactive Children's Support Group, Dr Stephen Davies, Dr Damien Downing, Dr Vicky Rippere, Dr M. J. Radcliffe, Dr Stanley Newman, Professor Bryce-Smith, Reading University, Dr Martin Herbert, Leicester University, Mr David Potterton, Mrs Sam Westmacott, Mr Beswetherick, Mrs Jane Thurnell-Read, Pauline Price and Mary Alcock of Basingstoke 'Helpline', Teresa Bliss of the Reading Hyperactive Support Group, and Graham Ledger, producer/presenter, Radio 210.

Thanks for additional help received through correspondence from Dr James Dobson, Dr John Upledger, Mr Harold Klug, Mr Simon Fielding, Mrs Wendy Simmonds, Mr Peter Campbell, Mrs Nim Barnes, Mr and Mrs Norman and Ruth Jervis.

Very special thanks to Janne Marie Bunker, artist, for her delightful illustrations; to Richard Hackett for photographs of Tanya as a young child; to Jim Gilford for the more recent photos and those of the other children; and to Tessa Harrow, my editor, for her helpful advice during the writing of this book.

Acknowledgment is also made to Tyndale House Publishers, for the abstract from the book *The Strong-Willed Child*, by

James C. Dobson; Turnstone Press Ltd, for permission to quote from *Allergies – Your Hidden Enemy* by Theron Randolph; Radio 210 for permission to quote from the 'What's Up Doc?', on Hyperactive Children; Dr David Horrobin, for permission to quote from his work; Ellen G. White Estate, for permission to quote from the books, *Ministry of Healing* and *Counsels on Diets and Foods*; Dr Stephen Davies for permission to quote from his lecture taped by Inter-Forum; *Nursing Times*, for permission to quote from the article 'Daniel's Allergies'.

Introduction

Writing this book has been a revelation to me; my life will never be quite the same again. I began writing with the intention of telling other people what it is like to live with a hyperactive child, through the story of my own daughter and through interviews with parents of children experiencing similar difficulties. The interviews with medical and educational personnel, and the comments of self-help groups, are designed to show parents that something can be done and explain how to go about finding the help they require – it is not simply a case of having to live with the problem and hoping that as the child grows up it will 'go away'. To my great surprise, however, it was while researching for this book that I also found the answer to the problems that had plagued my husband for most of his life, and were growing worse! But I will tell you about this later.

Finding a solution is very important for parents with one (or more) hyperactive children growing up within their home. It is not sufficient for them to be told by their doctor that most children grow out of it before they reach their teens. In the meantime family life is made difficult, if not impossible, marriages are stretched to breaking point, and relationships with other relatives and friends become frayed at the edges, if not abandoned. The child suffers from rejection by other children and is often punished very severely by his parents in their attempt to make him behave more acceptably; he finds school a terrible trial because he cannot sit still and behave and has difficulty in learning, does not get on well with his peers, is unable to do what is expected of him and so learns to be a failure. And if he does not grow out of it – what then? Parents faced with a teenager who is impulsive and aggressive have a much bigger problem to deal with than a two year-old who swings from the curtains and falls off the bookshelf. And it is more difficult to experiment on a teenager with behaviour improvement strategies, or to alter his eating habits. He has reached an age when he has rights and resents interference from adults.

What do we mean by hyperactivity – or, as it is also called, hyperkinesis, minimal brain dysfunction, attention deficit disorder, among many other terms? All children are full of life and naughty at times, particularly when parents want them to be on their best behaviour. Hyperactivity is a symptom which indicates that, somewhere in the child's make-up, there is something organically or functionally wrong. It is not just a matter of a child who is very active. There are numerous things which upset him and cause problems. In addition to being overactive, such children cry a great deal, have problems with sleep, become angry or depressed; they may be very clumsy, find it difficult to concentrate, speak too much or have difficulty in communicating; they sometimes dislike being touched, may think of themselves as stupid or that other people dislike them, and so on. Parents or teachers of hyper-active children are usually fairly certain that something is radically wrong. Other people who do not see the child very often may volunteer the information that 'he is just a normal healthy child'. It is unlikely that they would feel the same way given sole charge of him for a while.

Where does the answer lie? Drugs are one solution offered to parents seeking help. It has been found that stimulant drugs have a paradoxical effect on hyperactive children, temporarily calming them down. But the use of drugs is merely papering over the cracks: the problem still exists and is merely obscured for a short time. Besides, drug taking is fraught with possible dangers – side effects, drug dependence, and damage to the child through long-term use.

Help for the child can often be found through behaviour modification. The parents can be taught by a psychologist to use these skills which are merely a more consistent use of the rules they normally apply to discipline children. The services of an educational psychologist can help the child, his teachers and parents, with problems which arise at school, and will also test his actual ability. This is important to all concerned, as many hyperactive children are of average or above average ability and yet are under-achieving, sometimes having to attend special schools for the educationally subnormal (ESN) because normal schools cannot cope with them.

Then there is diet. What are we feeding our children? Chemicals, colourings, preservatives, junk food, food with little nutritional value! The removal of these, and their replacement with good nourishing food minus the additives and colours, produces startling results in many children. Some children, too, are found to be allergic to certain foods, and when these are isolated the child's attitude alters and his personality has a chance to blossom. Lead pollution can have far-reaching effects on human beings. It finds its way into the brain and remains there, altering the ability to control behaviour. The organisation Foresight was established to study such problems and to endeavour to prevent them before they occur by preparing parents prior to the conception of a child, so that their own health is in peak condition before they create a new life. Special osteopathic treatment soon after birth can relieve damage caused to the infant's head during birth and can also help older children. Finally, medical herbalists can offer relief by practical means.

So it is not just a case of 'having to live with it' or 'he will grow out of it'. There are positive things that can be done and the earlier the better, before the child and his family and all concerned have had to suffer too long or additional problems have arisen.

PART ONE

Bringing up a Hyperactive Child

1 Early Days

The birth
The long months of waiting had at last come to an end. I had
enjoyed a beautiful pregnancy with no problems at all; even
morning sickness had not troubled me too much in the early
months. As I helped the children to dress each morning at the
Children's Home where I worked, the smell of breakfast
cooking had made me feel distinctly uncomfortable, but the
first mouthful of cereal dismissed the nausea. I loved being
pregnant but, like any mother-to-be, longed for the day when I
could hold my own child in my arms. Now at last, after a blur of
hours in labour, I could see my baby. I gazed for the first time
at the strange being lying on my body, looking much larger and
quite different from what I had imagined. It lay perfectly still
and apparently lifeless. No one spoke. The thought 'still-born'
came into my mind and refused to leave. A nurse picked up the
baby and removed it from my sight.

I lay watching the large clock on the wall. During labour its
hands had appeared to spin round, registering hours in the
space of minutes as I slept and woke again, as contractions
came and went. Now the hands barely moved and the minutes
hung like hours. Then suddenly I heard the sound that I had
been praying for but had begun to fear I would never hear:
my baby's cry. It was not long and lusty, more like a tired
whimper, but it was sufficient to reassure me that my baby
lived.

Following this reassurance I ventured to ask, 'What is it, a
girl or a boy?'

'Oh, I'm SO sorry,' said the doctor. 'Didn't we tell you? It's
a girl!'

What a relief! My baby alive – and a GIRL! Tanya – our own

little miracle with us at last. To give birth to a baby girl had always been the height of my ambition. Not that I would have rejected a boy; in fact during the last weeks of pregnancy I had called 'it' by a boy's name and put away the hope that it would be a girl.

Very soon the moment arrived for me to sit up in bed nursing Tanya in my arms for the first time. It was an experience impossible to describe. I wanted to cry for joy as I looked into her beautiful eyes, played with her tiny fingers and toes and admired her wispy hair.

Before the birth of a child most parents have a mental image of what their child will be like and what they will do together as the baby grows and develops. My picture of the future was coloured by memories of my own childhood. I envisaged taking my baby out in a pram for walks in the country. Before long she would be able to sit up and I could introduce her to the beautiful world of trees, flowers, birds, animals, streams and lakes. Soon she would walk and we would enjoy wandering down footpaths and making paper boats to sail on the streams. She would sit on my lap and listen to stories and we would sing songs together. Her father would teach her to play the piano and perhaps she would learn the violin, too. These dreams had made me impatient for her birth. Hidden away inside my body she was missing so much. But at last she had been compelled to leave her cramped quarters to explore the world with me.

Getting acquainted

We chose the name Tanya because it was unusual – or so we thought! The day after her birth I discovered that the newborn baby in the next cot had the same name. Then the next mum-to-be to join us in the ward announced, 'If it's a boy it'll be Sion and if it's a girl, Tanya.' Sion arrived during the night.

Tanya was born on January 4th to face a countryside covered with ice and snow. My mother-in-law slipped and slithered to the hospital every afternoon to visit her first precious grandchild, and my parents made the long trip from the North to savour their first experience of being grandparents. Marie-Luise, a German teenager staying with us for a year to learn English, would call in during the afternoons and sit knitting

beside my bed before rushing off to her evening classes at the college in the next town. My husband, Leslie, now a proud father, came during the evenings to sit and admire the little scrap swathed in a soft sheet. We all began to know her in the next few days.

All the babies in the ward slept and fed well; only the other Tanya caused difficulties. She was a big, bald, bouncing baby always yelling for a feed, but doted on by her elegant seventeen year-old mother and young father. We received very little advice about breast feeding and I began to run into problems. Most of the mothers spent their time discussing their other children at home, their husbands or their postnatal discomforts. We had an outbreak of 'tummy bug' which sent us one by one into temporary isolation. Then workmen arrived to repair the ceiling. This called for a general move from the main ward for twenty-four hours.

Learning to cope

After ten days Tanya and I were released from the artificial world of the maternity ward to fend for ourselves at home. It worried me a great deal that I had been unable to continue breast feeding. Lacking advice, when the milk supply proved inadequate we went home to bottle feeding, contrary to plans, and once there Tanya fed slowly, only consuming an ounce of milk before falling asleep. In an hour or so she would wake crying, and she often regurgitated her feed. I felt as weak as a kitten and tired out from trying to cope with sleepless nights, nappies, bottles, washing and cooking – just some of the usual problems faced by all young mothers with a new baby.

But one thing seemed unusual and marked the beginning of Tanya's constant restlessness: she did not nestle to my body as I fed her, instead pushing away and arching her back. Each time I fed her this worsened, until she would feed only with her head hanging down backwards and her back arched over my knees – not the recommended position for feeding a baby! Before she was two months old I decided that it would be preferable to sit her up in a baby chair to feed her. This solved the problem, although I missed the close relationship between us as I fed her. As she grew a little older she struggled to get out of her chair at meal times by sliding down as far as she could. In doing so she

rubbed the back of her legs on the chair so hard that, on several occasions, she removed the skin.

Until she was well over two years of age she rejected my attempts to cuddle her and wriggled constantly in an apparent attempt to reach the floor long before she could walk, yet when I laid her on a rug on the floor she was unhappy. She would not stay on the rug once she had learnt to roll off it, becoming trapped under the furniture, whereupon she would begin to scream. Nor did she show much interest in toys placed near her. She did not want to sit up when able to do so and until she reached eleven or twelve months preferred to remain lying down in her pram; if I propped her up so that she could see around her, she simply slid down again. The transfer to the push chair made it more difficult for her to do this, but she did not like being put in it and screamed when strapped in, struggling to get out. She had to be firmly secured in the pushchair or she would not have remained in it.

Pre-walking stage
The difficulties we encountered with Tanya as a small baby

paled into insignificance as she grew more mobile. We were as
eager as any parents to encourage her to stand and walk, and a
baby walker seemed an ideal way of helping her towards in-
dependence. It proved to be a somewhat mixed blessing; when
first introduced to it she tried to lie back in it rather than sit up
and obviously had no idea how to push with her feet to make it
move. After a few sessions in it she began to enjoy sitting up
and viewing the world from a new vantage point and this kept
her amused for short periods. Then she learned to push with
her feet and managed to move backwards. This taste of success
brought forth ideas for new adventures: she discovered that
she could propel herself wherever she wished and then stand up
in the walker and reach objects hitherto beyond her grasp; her
ability to manoeuvre her walker backwards and forwards
increased daily and she managed to reach objects placed further
from the edge of surfaces and higher up. She seemed delighted

with this new-found freedom and dashed around the room grabbing whatever she could reach and breaking or tearing it. She took no notice when told 'No' or given a slap for destroying other people's things; finally we just moved everything well out of reach and decided that she would learn as she grew older what she could have and what she was not allowed to touch. Unfortunately she did not learn; she developed into the obnoxious child who enters someone else's home and dives into drawers and cupboards and picks things up from shelves.

Tanya then discovered new tricks. She found that she could propel herself at great speed across the room in her baby walker. She would kick off from the window end, fly across the room and crash into the door at the other end. This soon led to disaster as she tried to break her own record and became more and more reckless, leaning forward as she sped across the room until eventually she fell out of the walker onto her head. This happened time and again, so the walker had to be put away.

The daily round

Almost two years before Tanya's birth we had moved to the Cotswolds, to a delightful stone house typical of that area of England. It was several hundred years old and had been partially modernised. It looked charming but was not ideal for bringing up children. The kitchen had a fireplace in the corner of the room; this, when lit, was of little use for heating the whole room and it was impossible to sit near it as the door from the hall opened back across it. The house, pleasantly cool in summer, became cold and draughty in the winter. It had very thick walls and wide window sills; as the windows opened outwards these made dangerous seats, particularly upstairs, and eventually we had bars fitted to the windows to prevent accidents.

At the time we did not know how fortunate we were that, after the first few months, Tanya slept well at night. Many children like Tanya are overactive both by day and by night. I always put her to bed at a regular time and once asleep we could be sure of peace until the morning. This was such a relief; if she had been as active at night as she became during the day I would have been unable to cope. I have always needed a good night's sleep and am useless without it. The fact that she slept well allowed me time to recharge my batteries in order to cope with her the following day, for by now she needed constant attention to prevent her screaming or getting into danger or difficulties. Housework became impossible. For example, I would try to make the bed in my own room: if I put her on the floor, in no time she would have all the books out of the bookcase near the bed; if I put her on the divan in the corner of the room with some toys, she would fall off and begin to scream; if I put toys on the floor for her she would abandon them and climb onto a chest of drawers and thence onto the window sill. As a last resort, I tried sitting her on the bed as I made it, but as fast as I straightened the bedclothes she would fling them about. So I buried any pride I might have had in my house and left the housework until after her bedtime.

Feelings of incompetence

By now I had begun to feel rather inadequate both as a housewife and a mother. I had always had success with children and babies and had prided myself on my ability to care for them. If a baby would not sleep I could lull it into slumber in no time; little ones always responded well to me and mothers had trusted me with their babies and toddlers from the time I myself was a child. I had worked with physically handicapped children, some of whom were also mentally handicapped, and had coped well with any problems that arose. Yet here in my own home with my own child I felt at a loss to deal with the situation. Also I felt less than a woman. Each day became a struggle for existence; there seemed to be no time for me to think of my own needs and I longed to be able to take a little time to do my hair nicely and care for my skin. Intellectually I suffered as I no longer had time to read or discuss any topic of interest, local, political or religious. One day I remember escaping from the situation and leaving Leslie to cope with his daughter for a short while (as he worked long hours he felt less geared up when at home to deal with her than I did). I retreated to the spare bedroom and sat on the window sill watching the rain pouring down on the road below, and just allowed the silence to engulf me.

Reorganisation

In order to make cooking possible I fixed a baby gate between the larger kitchen and the tiny room which housed the cooker and sink. This proved to be an invaluable aid. As I have never had aspirations to be a *cordon bleu* cook, I concentrated on meals which were filling but not fancy and very quick to prepare, meanwhile keeping an eye on Tanya in the adjoining room. She enjoyed watching me through the gate and it kept her away from the danger of the saucepans on the cooker. It was sometimes possible to do the washing with Tanya safely on the other side of the gate, but as she grew older and even more demanding this too became an occupation for the evenings.

We rarely stayed in during the afternoons. Once lunch had been cleared away we would don our outdoor clothes and go to visit a neighbour whose baby had been born a few days after Tanya. Helen and I had attended prenatal relaxation classes together and we enjoyed meeting every day to take our babies for a walk. Helen's little lad seemed so placid compared with Tanya; he played happily with his toys, sat up long before Tanya and walked at ten months. Although Helen had little to say, we mothers got on together far better than our children. Tanya was not averse to biting the little boy or hitting him with his toys, so we usually took them out in their prams to the swings or the village shop, or walked around the country lanes. It really helped to have someone to meet, even though her child was so totally different from mine.

Tanya learns to walk

As Tanya neared her first birthday she had not yet learned to crawl in the conventional way, but if held by me at one end of the room would run when released and crash into her father's arms at the other end. She seemed in too much of a hurry to take careful steps and learn to balance. When she reached fourteen months, I took her for a short visit to her grandparents in Wales; suddenly one day she stood up and walked from one room to the other with no trouble at all. On returning home she went down onto her knees and crawled everywhere for about a week and then began to walk again. We laughed about this. Tanya just had to be different – running first, walking next and learning to crawl last!

Nothing seemed impossible for Tanya now that she could walk. She would push chairs across the room in order to reach the objects that we had placed out of reach – nothing was safe. She raced from one mischief to the next in a frenzied attempt to find something of interest, and, as fast as she found something to play with, suitable or not, she would abandon it and race on to pick up, drop, move or break something else. This happened both inside and outside the house. When walking a few paces behind me one day near the village church, she found and began to eat yew berries. Fortunately she seemed to dislike the taste and spat them out rather than swallow them. Another day she found a packet of weed killer left behind by a previous tenant in what we thought was a completely empty garage. The doctor showed concern, but again she had no ill effects and it may be that we caught her before she swallowed any, just managing to spill it down the front of her coat as she tried to eat it.

Whatever Tanya found to hold ceased to interest her after a few seconds, so it was impossible to amuse her in the normal way that one does a small child. She acted like a mechanical toy which has just been wound up and races madly in all directions. I found myself always one move behind her, picking up the pieces as she chased after something else. The best solution seemed to be to place piles of toys in the room so that she could run from object to object, thus keeping her amused for short periods of time. I so much wanted to become involved in her activity and be able to play with my child, but this did not seem possible. She disliked sitting on my lap and attempts to show her picture books failed dismally.

By now Helen's baby had learnt to play constructively with simple toys and his parents enjoyed sharing activities with him. If his father dug the garden, Richard came out with his toy spade and copied him or tried to pull up the weeds. He would amuse himself for hours digging in his sand pit while his father worked in the garden. The more I tried to build up this kind of relationship with Tanya the more frustrated I became and the more difficult to manage she seemed.

Out of doors
During the summer months we spent a great deal of time in the

open air. Fortunately we had a large paddock behind our house and a garden beyond that, so we had plenty of space in which Tanya could play. She had a small bike, a 'sit on and push' toy, a truck filled with large bricks, a pram and dolls and a teddy bear. If only a few things were available she quickly became bored, so each time I brought all the toys into the garden and she could move from toy to toy as she wished. I sat on a rug and watched her the whole time to make sure that she came to no harm. Without my prompting she would come over to see me now and again to have a romp and then run off again at high speed. I began to count my blessings that we did not live in a high-rise flat or in a house with no garden.

Now that Tanya could walk we were limited in the distance we could go from home. She did not want to be confined to her push chair, but neither did she want to walk any distance. In fact she hated walking. On a short walk she ran around like a small puppy – ahead, behind and round and round, tiring herself out before we reached the end of the road. Then she cried from exhaustion, wanted to be carried – but only for a few yards – and did not really want to sit in her push chair. These outings were fraught with peril, too – she seemed to have no sense of danger whatsoever. When we reached the village green where cars passed more frequently, I had to keep her close to me to prevent her running into the road; she resented this very much. A stream ran through the village and she had no fear of falling into it. When I tried to make a phone call at the kiosk she would not sit outside in her push chair, but if I took her into the kiosk she ate the cigarette ends off the floor, so I had to sit her on the parcel shelf. To prevent her falling off I held her with one hand while trying to dial the number I required. If she could get one of her arms free she reached out and pressed the rest, thus disconnecting my call. At the same time she screamed and cried to get out of the kiosk.

The shopkeeper in the village loved children. If he picked Tanya up and stood her on the counter she would fall backwards expecting him to catch her, regardless of whether he was behind her or not. The first time she did this it gave him quite a fright as none of his other little customers had ever done this, and he almost missed her.

The hazards of car rides

Most children enjoy riding in a car and Tanya was
exception, but the trips had to be short. As a small baby
motion of the car soon sent her to sleep, but when she gre
little older she very quickly became bored, unless she was ti
enough to fall asleep. Marie-Luise, our German friend, st
remembers how she used to let Tanya play with her long hair
we drove to Oxford each week, rather than have her screamin
all the way. Sometimes Tanya pulled it quite hard and Marie
Luise ended up with a sore head!

We bought a child's car seat and this proved very useful. She
never found out how to open the belt and anyway it needed an
adult's strength to turn the catch. This kept her safe in the car
and we always used it whether or not someone sat in the back
seat with her. Had she sometimes been allowed to sit
unconfined in the back of the car she would have resented
sitting in the seat at other times – where Tanya was concerned
we learned the wisdom of keeping fairly strictly to routine. As
soon as she entered the car she began leaping up and down and
doing somersaults over the seats, so without the car seat it
would have been impossible for me to drive anywhere alone
with her.

A long journey

Before Tanya reached two years of age my husband had the
offer of a job in Cornwall. It was necessary for both of us to see
what was offered as the job would involve me as well, and when
we were invited to stay for a week we decided to make the visit
our holiday. The journey was a long one, but we left early and
planned to eat picnics on the way and have a number of breaks.
We set off and Tanya fell asleep for a short while. When she
woke she quickly became tired of the journey and began to
scream. Leslie went to sit in the back of the car with her, but
she would not be amused by him or her toys. After a while we
stopped and had a walk and she became happy once again, but
as soon as we walked towards the car she began to cry. We had
to fight with her to put her back into the car seat and continued
our journey with Tanya crying. Nothing interested her or
consoled her; her screams grew louder and louder until I could
not concentrate on driving. We stopped several times for

another walk, and each time we had the same struggle to get her back into the car seat. I hated having to slap her to make her sit down but there was nothing else to do; we could not afford to stay anywhere overnight, we had to continue our journey, and she would not sit still in the car without being in her seat. The journey turned into a nightmare. We travelled for about an hour at a time with stops in between, but seemed to be making little progress towards Cornwall. Our heads spun with tiredness and the noise. Finally, hours late and long after dark, we arrived in Cornwall.

We had been promised a cot for Tanya, but on arrival we were told that it had not been found and that our hostess would make up a bed for her on the floor. However, tired as she was, she would not sleep and kept getting up and walking around. Finally she fell asleep, allowing us to get some rest, but as dawn broke she awoke and began jumping all over us. We went through this ritual every day that week. With the lack of a good night's sleep and the effect of the sea air we felt worn out by the time we left, dreading the homeward journey, our courage screwed up to face the screaming. As soon as we left, however, Tanya fell asleep. We were almost afraid to stop at traffic lights in case she woke, but she slept on for most of the journey. We drove along hardly daring to believe in our good fortune and the miles seemed nothing while peace reigned in the car. When Tanya awoke we were not too far from home. Because she had slept so long she quite enjoyed the rest of the journey. At least the lack of sleep during the week had served some good purpose.

We enjoyed our visit to Cornwall, meeting new friends, seeing new places, but vowed that, if we went again, we would either stay overnight on the way or leave Tanya behind. In the event, the job we had gone to discuss proved to have snags and did not work out, so we had no need to make the journey again.

Tanya did not begin to enjoy car rides of more than ten or fifteen minutes until she was much older. However, she always preferred a ride in the car to going for a walk, and we found it difficult to go for a walk as a family because she disliked walking for more than a short distance. It took the joy out of a stroll in the country or through the woods to have a child crying and moaning, wanting to be carried, wanting to go home, and being generally miserable. One would have expected that a child with so much energy to expend would be glad of the chance to walk, but not Tanya.

Shopping

While Tanya was a small baby, the village shop supplied most of our requirements, and as I had a carry cot with wheels as well as her large pram, visits to the local town were no hardship. Before she could walk I used a push chair and this, too, was reasonably easy. However, after she found her feet the problems grew. I would get out of the car and, with Tanya wearing reins for safety, go to the first shop. If our visit there did not last too long all would be well, but by the time we entered the second shop the trouble had begun; she had used up all her patience by then and wanted to go home. I remember one day in particular: at the second shop, Tanya tried to grab articles off the shelves and when I restrained her she began to cry. As I waited at the cash desk she fought to reach more goods off the shelves and because I prevented this, she lay down on the shop floor and screamed as if I had been beating her. Everyone began to stare at us; I could almost read their thoughts as they glared at me:

'Spoilt little brat. Fancy letting her carry on like that.'

'Some people have no idea how to bring up a child.'

'Poor little thing. Whatever have you done to make her scream like that?'

The problems with shopping did not ease as Tanya grew older, for she had no fear of getting lost. As I battled with my shopping she was constantly on the move, so that I spent more time trying to hold onto her, or looking for her, than in actual shopping. When she ran away, it did not worry her in the least that she could not see me and did not know where to find me; if she became lost she did not even bother to look for me. This of course was potentially very dangerous, with the risk that she might run out into the road, go away with someone or just become completely lost. My visits to the town therefore became less frequent and I relied more and more on the village shop, with short visits to the town for specific things. In the village I left my list with the shopkeeper one day and picked it

up and paid for it the next day, with no trouble whatsoever. What did it matter if everything cost a little more than in the supermarket? I had saved the petrol and used up far less nervous energy.

2 Growing Problems

Naming the problem

This situation might have gone on, becoming worse and worse with my having no idea why Tanya acted so differently from expectations. Fortunately a doctor at the group practice had a particular interest in child development. When she was about two and a half years old I received a request to visit the surgery for Tanya to be given child development tests. All children born in the practice were having them if the parents did not object. I took Tanya along, feeling quite interested to see what tests she would have and how she would respond. The doctor welcomed us and began to show Tanya what he wanted her to do, but the objects on his desk held no interest for her at all. She raced across the room, climbed onto the window seat and grabbed some dolls. She ran back to me and then returned to the window seat. I fetched her back and the tests began. The doctor succeeded in getting her to perform some of the tasks he set her, but she really wanted to be elsewhere. After several abortive attempts to continue the doctor looked at me and said,

'She is hyperactive. Would you like a social worker to call and see you to give you some help with her?'

I knew very little about social workers at this time and declined his offer. I felt that we had worked out our own ways of keeping her fairly well under control and had reservations about another person arriving on the scene to 'help'. Later I regretted this decision, as someone to share a problem is often invaluable.

As I returned home his words kept ringing in my ears – 'She is hyperactive . . .' We knew that she was not at all easy to deal with – we often felt that we were failing in her upbringing – but now the doctor had given us a name which summed it up: 'hyperactive'. Nothing had changed, both she and I were the same, but now I felt strangely relieved that someone else had recognised that things were not quite right. I felt able to look at the problem and cope with it better now that it had been defined.

A brother for Tanya

We had never intended to have only one child. My parents had married rather late in life, so I had no brothers and sisters; Leslie's sister had died at six months as she had an enlarged liver and when, five years later, he was born, his parents, too, were no longer young; so we had both missed the experience of having brothers and sisters. I felt that it had been more difficult to grow up and learn to relate to people without other children in my family, while Leslie had been very lonely and had clung to his mother as a small child because he had no children to play with at home. We planned to have at least two children, but as we experienced the problems that Tanya presented, we decided to wait until she reached school age before embarking on providing her with a companion. In that way I would be able to rest a little in the later months of pregnancy whilst she attended school. However something happened which changed our plans.

We had become interested in fostering when Tanya was nearly a year old, although we did little about it until a social worker visited the Seventh-day Adventist Church in Oxford which we attended each week. At the Toy Service she asked the congregation if any parents would be interested in fostering a child. We and another family volunteered at once. Some months later, after careful vetting, we were registered as foster parents. We had two children to care for briefly whilst their mother went abroad to visit relatives and then we waited for months and months. As we lived in the country we were not near enough to the town to be dropped on in emergencies by the social worker seeking short term care for children late at night, or with little or no warning.

Eventually we met John through a friend who worked at a Children's Home. He needed a foster home and we were registered foster parents, so it did not take us long to get together. John moved in to share our hearts and our home. At four and a half it must have been quite difficult for him to adjust to a new mum and dad and a very lively little sister of two. He seemed to take it all in his stride, although for years Tanya liked to prove that she had the upper hand. For the first couple of days we wondered if we had taken on too much. John rushed around from one thing to another in a similar way to Tanya. However this quickly subsided as he found his way around. We found that he became as slow to move around as Tanya was quick.

John's arrival in the family helped Tanya considerably. Although she had begun to speak around the usual time, she had lost interest in speech because she was always racing around. John, however, had a great deal to say for himself. After all, he had experienced changes in his life which normally happen only to adults. He needed to express himself and to establish relationships. This spurred Tanya on to speak. For months she referred to him as 'Boy' and her favourite statement became, 'Come here, Boy!' John needed a lot of physical affection to make up for what he had missed and to reassure him that he belonged to his new family. Seeing John being cuddled, for the first time in her life Tanya sought us out for affection. True, her embraces were rather brief, but at least it showed a move in the right direction. She did not become really thoughtfully affectionate until ten years of age.

The attic
Our Cotswold home had two bedrooms on the first floor and two further rooms in the attic. Tanya was still sleeping in her cot when John arrived, so we moved it up into the attic, leaving John the bedroom on the first floor. Despite the fact that her cot had a low level for the mattress to keep the child in the cot, she had learnt the art of climbing out earlier than we had thought possible. She usually slept in the mornings until someone got up; then, at the first sound, she would wake and want to be up and about. John tended to wake early but kept himself amused by 'reading' his picture books until asked to get up. He began to wake earlier and earlier and Tanya could hear him as soon as he started to 'read' (he sometimes mistook night for day and began his early morning session in the middle

of the night – he seemed surprised when I rushed in to put the light out and get him back to sleep).

As I did my housework at night when the children had gone to bed, I needed all the rest I could get and felt unable to leap up early and greet the day with enthusiasm. Tanya was quite safe up in the attic; she could not open the door, the window was high off the floor with no sill and there was nothing else in the room but her cot and a rug. To keep her amused until I could summon up the strength to face the day, I placed toys and books in and near the cot, and from my room I could hear what she was doing. She would amuse herself by looking briefly at a few books and mutilating the rest (old catalogues came in useful), and by playing for a short while with the other toys, before the noises from above told me that she had had enough of being alone. I loved her dearly but had to pluck up courage to climb the attic stairs to fetch her. I needed to be fully awake and alert before I brought her down, as it took a great deal of concentration to cope with her changing moods and flying feet all day long.

Getting lost
John soon began school in the village. A neighbour and I took it in turns to walk with the children to school, as it involved crossing the main road through the village along which cars often drove too fast. Tanya liked to take John to school when it was our turn, but sometimes I had not dressed her by school time and then my husband, who worked across the road, would look after her for me for the few minutes it took to walk to the school and back. He watched her for me on one particular morning when she wanted to come with me and was cross at being left behind. When I returned I dressed her ready to go out to play in the paddock while I washed the breakfast dishes; this normally kept her amused until I was free to be with her. After a few seconds there was an ominous silence, so I went outside to find her. She did not appear to be in the paddock and a quick glance into the garden beyond revealed nothing. I ran to the corner of the road which led to the school, but there was no sign of Tanya. 'Perhaps she has gone to the swings,' I thought. I grabbed my bicycle and rode to the village green just down the road. No child there. To her father, then? I quickly

found him, but he had not seen her. To Lou's house where her friends lived? No, she had not seen her either. Perhaps I should go right to the school? I headed in that direction, thinking of the cars on the road nearby. En route I saw the young woman who lived opposite the school driving towards me, and in her car sat Tanya. She had been found wandering in the playground of the school. What a relief to find her unharmed! Obviously I could not afford to let her out of my sight if she could disappear so fast.

On another day, Tanya was in the kitchen with some toys, the baby gate across the doorway as usual, while I cleaned up in the smaller room. Tanya ceased to make any sound and I could not believe that she would be sitting perfectly still and quiet. I climbed over the gate and found that the door to the hall stood slightly ajar; she must have grown the fraction which allowed her to reach and turn the handle. The hall and sitting room were empty; so were both bedrooms and the tiny bathroom – surely she could not have climbed into the attic? The steep ladder-like stairs took skill to negotiate and I usually carried her up and down them. There was no sign of her in the first attic room and her own room appeared to be empty.

Panic began to rise in me as I retraced my steps and searched each room again more carefully. Surely she had not gone out of the front door? It took an adult's strength to lift the heavy latch and pull open the sticking door. I checked it, just in case, but it stood tightly shut. I climbed back to the attic – still no sign. As I paused for a second to reconsider the situation a slight movement of Tanya's cot eiderdown caught my eye. Impossible! Small as she was I should be able to see the shape of her body under the cover. I moved forward and raised the corner of the eiderdown. There she lay, for once as quiet as a mouse, in her hand a pack of aspirins. The relief of having found her faded as I picked her up and noticed that she had opened the pack. She had managed to break into several of the 'bubbles' but in doing so the tablets had broken and most of them lay in her cot uneaten; the little she had taken did her no harm. Even I could not believe that she had moved so quickly, negotiated the attic stairs and climbed *into* her cot, with nothing to stand on to help her up and over the side. The pack of aspirins was a mystery too, since as far as I knew we had none

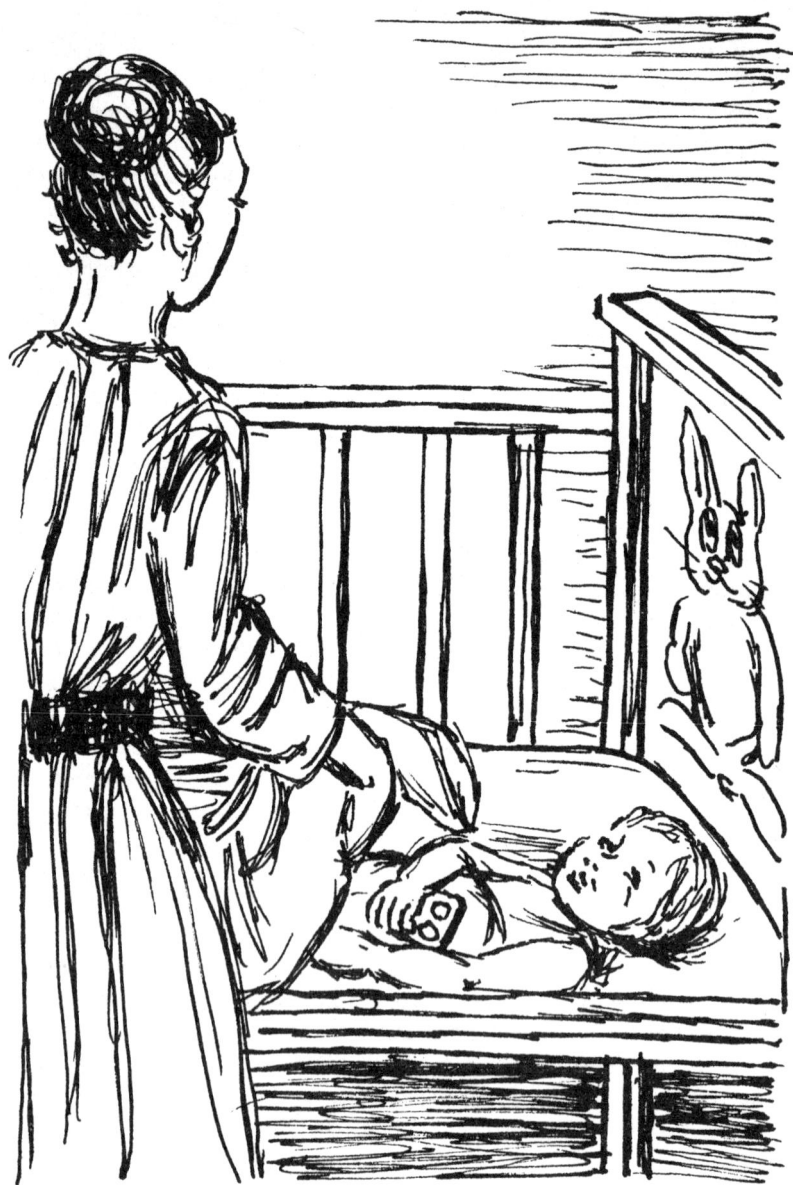

in the house, and I never found out where she had managed to find them.

These episodes made me very wary of allowing other people to look after Tanya. If she could outwit me, how could I expect someone who knew little of her behaviour to keep her safe? When my parents-in-law visited it caused problems, as father in particular felt that I fussed far too much. When we went to the local town he allowed her to run ahead of him along the pavement. I ran to catch up with her and hold her hand, but he resented my interference, saying, 'She's all right with me.' I suggested that he hold her hand but he declined to do so. 'What if she runs into the road?' I ventured. 'Oh, she's all right. I can catch her.' I considered this highly unlikely and felt terribly uneasy the whole time we were in the town, hovering ready to grab her myself if she made a suicidal leap into the road. I had to try to strike a balance between keeping the peace with father-in-law and making sure that Tanya came to no harm.

Later, when he played hide and seek with her at home, I tried to mention, very casually, that she might run out into the road beside our house. 'Don't you worry, she is fine with me. I'll look after her,' he said. I left them to play but went through the house and out into the road, just in time to catch Tanya as she ran full pelt out into the road from the side entrance. As it happened there were no vehicles in sight, but the chance of a passing car missing her as she ran straight out was rather slim.

I began to ponder the question, 'Am I a neurotic mother?' Some parents on the estate up the road let their children out after breakfast and did not expect to see them again until lunch – and they came to no harm. But they stayed near home and played with other children in the cul-de-sac. Perhaps the fact that I always protected her made her less aware of danger and anxious to break away from my care?

One place that Tanya found to run to held less danger. One summer we had very good weather and I would dress her each morning in a cotton dress, cardigan, pants, shoes and socks. Within seconds of going out into the garden she had shed cardigan, pants, socks and shoes, leaving them scattered behind her as she fled. The dress remained on, as she could not undo the back fastening. Each time I found her on the swing in my neighbour's garden, with a visiting father pushing her to and fro. To reach their garden she had to climb through the barbed wire fence which had nettles in abundance on our side. I myself found it difficult to climb through to fetch her and I never managed to catch her to see how she avoided being stung or scratched. I often wondered what the man thought of a mother who sent a child out wearing only a dress! I never became well enough acquainted with him to explain the situation, as he only occasionally visited his daughter and son-in-law for a few weeks.

Without pants Tanya avoided the problem of accidentally wetting them. She was not easy to toilet train and remained rather unpredictable even after she went to school. If she happened to be too far from the toilet at the wrong moment an accident ensued, and the spare pants kept at school came in handy on many occasions. At night she had sporadic lapses until almost nine years of age, having come out of nappies at night when she was about three and a half.

Good health

During the years when Tanya was small I had good health, and this helped considerably. On one occasion, however, I had mild influenza, so for a couple of days I took Tanya into the spare bedroom with boxes of toys and books. The room contained a double divan, a chest of drawers, and a curtained wardrobe in the corner near the window. As the door was not easy to open, I could lie back in bed and allow Tanya to do whatever she liked. We just about survived, with her rolling to and fro across the bed, emptying and refilling boxes, falling off and leaping back onto the bed.

Tanya herself rarely had an illness which kept her in bed. However on two separate Christmasses she fell inexplicably ill, becoming very sleepy, not wanting to be bothered by anyone and feeling very content to sleep on the settee for most of the day. It came as a wonderful relief to the rest of us celebrating Christmas (our family and Leslie's parents); we could relax and talk without having to bother about Tanya's noisiness. We enjoyed a leisurely meal and it brought back to me memories of Christmasses past. Only parents of hyperactive children will

fully appreciate the relief from tension that we felt on those two Christmas days.

A family holiday

Once a year we aimed at having a holiday together, although with a child like Tanya a holiday could never be much of a rest. We could visit my parents in North Wales, but they found the disruption of their normally peaceful way of life quite a strain. The answer came through 'Family Camp'. We read about it in the church magazine and it sounded ideal. We booked to attend the Camp held in the North, at Aberdaron on the Lleyn Peninsula of North Wales. Travelling in that direction we could also call on my parents for a short visit before or after Camp. The accommodation consisted of a tent for each family, a main hall used for eating, indoor games, concerts, programmes and church services (it could also house all the campers in the event of the tents collapsing in a gale), flush toilets, hot and cold water, and a shower which either dribbled cold water or suddenly scalded the unsuspecting person. Each tent had light from an electric light bulb for a few hours every evening.

Each day began with a brief worship at the breakfast tables followed by routine duties and activities for the children for the whole of the morning. These included a play group for the under fives and various arts and crafts for the different age groups up to the teens. Parents could assist in any group, enjoy doing nothing for a change, drive to a nearby town, or go walking with an organised group.

After lunch all the families were invited to join a convoy of cars to drive to a different beach. Following the evening meal and worship, games of cricket, volley ball and table tennis went on until dark. Then baby minders began to walk around the site at regular intervals to alert any parents of crying babies or to scoop up exploring youngsters and return them to their mothers. In the main hall parents enjoyed discussion groups, games, a concert, or whatever the social committee (themselves campers) had planned.

For several years we went to Family Camp. It meant that each member of the family enjoyed a really good holiday and returned refreshed – indeed, the first year we went with Tanya

gave me a new lease of life. I left her each morning with the play group leaders and enjoyed the bracing walks and stimulating conversation of other adults. It was a tremendous relief to be able to relax and not have to watch her every second of the day. The mornings were a delight and the afternoons too were relaxed, with everyone keeping an eye on all the children as they made friends with each other and played together. There were so many things to occupy her that Tanya's behaviour improved. The first year we went to Camp, John and Tanya won the fancy dress competition dressed as Adam and Eve. I gave Tanya an apple to occupy her until their turn came to walk up to the platform. Once there, Tanya allowed John to take a bite of the apple which caused much laughter in the audience and seemed to sway the decision in their favour!

3 Medicine, Mishaps, Minding and Moving

The medicine

Soon after the doctor had suggested that Tanya was hyper-active, we had returned to the surgery to discuss the matter and to see what help might be available for us. He said that some children responded to drugs but that he did not recommend these as being in the long term beneficial to the child, although he felt that for the parents' sake they should sometimes be tried. He asked me what I did when Tanya played up really badly.

'When she is in a temper and totally refuses to be reasoned with, I take her to her room, shut her in and go downstairs. This gives me time to stand back and look at the situation and prevents me doing any harm to her,' I said. 'After a while she usually calms down and I feel able to cope again, so I bring her back down.' I did not know how the doctor would react to this but it was the truth and although I thought he might not approve, I told him anyway. To my surprise he thought this a good solution. For emergencies he suggested that we try Ospolot. He gave us a bottle to try with Tanya to see if it had any effect.

We tried the medicine but found that she needed frequent doses to make any difference in her behaviour. I tested it one day before I sent her to play group, dosing her regularly during the morning and then just before I left her at the play group. When I fetched her later the mother in charge for the day remarked on how quiet Tanya had been. Halfway through the session she thought: 'Tanya's not here today – but then I looked round and there she was, getting on quietly with the others. I could hardly believe it.' Although the Ospolot had this effect when sufficiently high amounts were given, we did not feel happy about constantly having to give her medicine to calm her down, as the effect wore off within an hour or so.

We were at Family Camp with Tanya during the summer when she reached three and a half years of age. I took the Ospolot with us as a standby but she did not really need it. There were plenty of things to do, people to see and wide open spaces to run around in, and all these novelties combined to minimise the problem for a while. I kept the medicine at the bottom of a bag with the top of the bag closed and placed it behind the suitcase in the tent, right out of the way.

Just before lunch one day, Tanya and a group of small children were playing on the swings in view of the main hall. Each family took it in turns to set tables, clear away and wash up after the meal and that day Leslie and I were on table setting. Seeing that Tanya had plenty to do, we tied up the tent and slipped quietly into the main hall. If she joined us there Leslie or I would have to stay with her to prevent her removing the cutlery as fast as we set the tables. We kept an eye on her while we worked. Then I realised that she had gone from the swings. I left Leslie to complete the job and went out to look for her across the field. Our tent had been opened a little. As I drew near, the man from the next tent met me with a bottle in his hand. He had seen Tanya enter the tent and knew that we were in the main hall. Being familiar with her behaviour, he looked in to see what she was doing and found her sitting in the middle of the tent pouring medicine into a spoon and drinking it. He had just taken it from her when I arrived. Fortunately she had not tried to drink directly from the bottle and in pouring the medicine into the spoon had spilt some onto the rug which we had spread on top of the ground sheet. Even so we could not account for about half the contents of the bottle.

We were not sure of the effect that the medicine would have on her and the camp nurse advised us to see the local doctor. He tried to make her vomit but she screamed and kicked so much that he could do little for her, so he arranged for us to take her to the nearest hospital, some forty miles away. En route we kept her awake with difficulty and gave her plenty to drink to dilute the medicine. At the hospital she disliked the doctor who examined her and screamed loudly. They decided to transfer her to another hospital in the town for observation.

We stayed there with her for the rest of the day and, as no ill effects were observed, we returned to camp in the evening. After that we did not feel inclined to use Ospolot or other drugs again.

Accident prone

The problem of Tanya's tendency to get into situations like this remained with us for years. We were geared up to the speed with which she could move, but even so, just when we thought that everything was under control, she could be into a dangerous situation in the space of seconds. Because of this we dared not relax for a second and felt it unsafe and unfair to leave her in the care of other people. As she grew older Leslie's parents managed to cope with her quite well for short holidays. They had the time to be with her all day, talking to her, playing with her, showing her new things and taking her out on interesting trips. However, my mother's response to looking after her was:

'Don't leave her with me. I'm accident prone and if she has an accident with me, I'd not forgive myself.'

This statement proved true on one visit. My mother took Tanya downstairs to show her something. She had the electric fire on in the kitchen. She went straight away and unplugged it because the flex lay stretched across the room and she did not want Tanya to trip over it or touch the hot fire. Shortly afterwards Tanya walked into the kitchen, tripped over her feet and sat on the electric fire. My mother picked her up at once, but the fire had not cooled down and the metal guard burned her leg and melted her nylon dress and slip. It really frightened my mother and reaffirmed her worst fears of being left to babysit.

Temporary additions

My neighbour had three little boys. Two were older than Tanya and the third younger. We became friendly when her third baby was on the way. I would take Tanya out in her pram and sit her second son on a pram seat so that she could have a rest on her own. As the children grew up I began to look after them now and again and she would occasionally mind Tanya for me. Then the arrangement became more permanent. She

would take her oldest boy and John to school and I would go to her house with Tanya and care for her two younger children.

This arrangement really suited Tanya. She loved to visit their home as they had different toys. For about an hour they would get all their toys out and play with them, then help to put them away. After a drink and biscuit in the kitchen while I finished clearing up the living room, they watched *Play School* on television while I gave the kitchen a quick clean. After the programme we put on our outdoor things and walked up the lane to my home. There I put a small trampoline in the kitchen, a box of toys and a pile of magazines. While I prepared the lunch the lads played happily with the toys and pretended that the trampoline was a boat, or a tractor, or whatever they fancied. Tanya became swept along by these activities and, because they lasted for a short time and the boys were so involved in their play, behaved reasonably well. After lunch, the swings on the village green were a favourite place to visit, with perhaps a quick visit to the shop. Very soon the time arrived to collect the two older boys from school. They were all tired by then and I became a familiar sight pushing Tanya's pushchair through the village with Tanya inside, my friend's youngest son sitting in front of her, the middle son perched on the hood and the two school boys trotting either side.

Although I felt tired after looking after this enlarged family each day, I felt much more fulfilled than when trying to cope with my own child by herself. The many changes in the day and the routine we had to follow in order to make it a workable proposition, helped her to be less of a problem. Seeing the other children engaged in an activity taught her how to play and the rapid change from one activity to another supplied her need for constant change.

Once more, close contact with other children showed up the differences between Tanya's behaviour and theirs. They had purpose in their play; they were inventive; they could concentrate for quite long periods; they asked intelligent questions; they could sit still for a while; they related to me; they wanted to show affection, enjoyed a cuddle and liked to hold my hand as we walked; most of all they loved listening to stories. At least once a week we lit the fire in my sitting room. The three boys and my son cuddled up around me in front of

the fire and listened while I read to them. In the meantime
Tanya came and went and showed little interest in the story.
My friend's sons were far from being little angels and of course
I had problems with them, as did their parents, yet despite this
the contrast was quite remarkable.

Moving house

Although we very much enjoyed living in the Cotswolds my
husband's job brought in little money. We lived in a tied house
and, even though we paid no rent or rates, we still had to eat
and heat the house. On the money he earned it became more
and more difficult to make ends meet. We had to run a car as
the village lay far from the large towns and quite a distance
from the smaller ones as well. Buses were few and far between.
Moreover, although we had thought about adopting John, we
did not have enough money to be accepted as able to keep him
unsupported. Leslie needed a good job with plenty of scope. In
the Cotswolds he had sole charge of a large private garden
which opened to the public once a year and also grew orchids
and subtropical plants. He needed to find a similar job but with
better pay. Then we had to consider the house offered with the
job. With Tanya racing around it had to be large enough and
with plenty of space out of doors.

We found what appeared to be the ideal place. On a private
road half a mile from the main road, it guaranteed safety for
children. The owner had two children of his own near in age to
ours. The bungalow we would have had a very large dining
room and an equally large kitchen, in addition to a small sitting
room and three bedrooms. An orchard and lawns surrounded
it and opposite were woods full of footpaths. The gardens of
the estate provided a lot of scope for Leslie and there were large
greenhouses. The money offered a good improvement but I
would also be required to help in the house on weekday
mornings. We tried in vain to find a play group that would
accept Tanya, but other parents who lived in the area had had
their names on the lists for months or years and we stood no
chance. There seemed only one possibility: a teacher who ran a
nursery school at her home. As the fees for this were more than
for the play groups there were fewer parents able to consider
sending their children to it. The owner of the estate offered to

pay for Tanya to attend so that I would be free to assist his wife. We moved in at the end of the summer and Tanya began attending the nursery school while John had a place at an excellent local school.

By the end of our first week we had just begun to settle in when the owner of the estate had a change of mind. Leslie returned to the bungalow before I left with the children for school.

'He has asked us to leave. He doesn't think I'm suitable for the job,' he told me in a state of shock.

We could not take it in – how could he possibly know that Leslie would not be suitable when he had hardly had time to do anything in the garden? We tried to point this out to the owner and he agreed to allow us to stay a little longer. However, the weather was dreadful, with torrential rain day after day making the ground sodden. The owner required Leslie to weed a huge border which had been neglected during the summer. You can imagine how difficult this proved in the pouring rain. Leslie tried to explain that gardeners keep off the soil in wet weather to avoid spoiling its structure, but the boss insisted that it must be done.

'Work in between showers,' he advised.

As the rain rarely stopped and the ground had been soaked by the previous days of rain, this advice proved useless. Each morning he came out to inspect.

'You have pulled up the weeds but you've left some roots. I want the roots up as well as I don't want them to grow again,' he said.

Leslie suggested that he concentrate on clearing out the sheds and preparing the greenhouses during the very wet weather. He did this and cleared up some paths on the edge of the woodland nearest to the main house. The rain continued and the boss kept on about the border and added the job of weeding the vegetable garden.

At the interview we had been under the impression that the owner required a gardener to run his estate. Leslie had been used to this; he would plan the work which needed to be done, discuss it with the owner and then carry it out according to the weather conditions and season. Now it seemed that the owner wished to run the estate and give Leslie the work to do in the order he suggested, regardless of conditions. He owned several factories and unfortunately seemed to expect his garden to be run in a similar manner. To add to the problems of the weather, one day the steering of the estate tractor went as Leslie was driving it. This did not help to improve the relationship between owner and gardener.

Just one month after we had moved in we received notice to leave. The wet weather continued. The devastating news had a very bad effect on the whole family. I sobbed on and off all day and Tanya and John became upset too. Leslie walked around in a state of shock. John's school sent someone to see us in the evening to see if any solution could be found. Meanwhile we sent off several letters in response to jobs advertised in gardening magazines. We felt helpless. We had moved to provide a better future for the family and now we were left with the prospect of being homeless and penniless. The next day Tanya woke feeling ill. We had begun to recover and to feel more optimistic, but the impact of seeing us so upset the day before now affected her physically. She ran a temperature and slept on and off throughout the day.

Miraculously we received the offer of another job with a house during that afternoon, in reply to our letters of the previous day. Mr Jones drove to see us and asked us to come and visit him the next day. The prospects there seemed quite good, but the house that went with the job had only two bedrooms. We did not really want John to have the problem of Tanya sharing a room with him and interfering with his possessions. He needed a room of his own, we felt, that he could retreat into away from Tanya's activities. But there we were – beggars cannot be choosers – we agreed to move after considering it and praying about it for a week. The wife at the previous estate still wanted me to work in the house, so this enabled us to keep the children at the same schools until places became available for them at a Church School slightly nearer our new home. My husband's job lasted for five years until we found it essential to move to provide the children with a bedroom each.

During the years when the children were without separate rooms they both suffered from a lack of space. Their room accommodated bunk beds and some storage space but left little

room to move. We could never find things and John became annoyed with Tanya for taking his belongings. He had to live with Tanya's mess and muddle which proved difficult to control in such a small space. She did not settle to sleep at night while she had big brother in the top bunk to annoy and they woke each other too early in the mornings. But we did have a large garden for them at this house and provided them with garden swings and plenty of outdoor toys.

4 Searching for Solutions

Tanya's problem continues
As she grew older Tanya's hyperactivity persisted and mealtimes began to be a problem. I had kept her in her baby chair for as long as I could, but once she grew out of it we had difficulty in keeping her at the table. 'Simple,' you may say, 'just sit her at the table and insist that she stays there.' It did not work out quite so easily. She sat at the table and ate a little, but she could not sit still. She sat, knelt, stood, climbed back onto her chair and fell off again. After that performance we would try again. Often the chair appeared to tip up and throw her onto the floor! She fell off her chair at least three times each mealtime if not more. As we ate we would suddenly look at each other and say, 'Where's Tanya?' She could move so fast that if one blinked she had disappeared from the table, and from the room as well. This sometimes caused problems between my husband and myself as we each wondered why the other had not seen her go and stopped her. In between trying to keep her at the table and in an upright position it seemed almost impossible for us to eat.

If she was not running away or falling off her chair she caused a commotion at the table, arguing, fighting with her brother or screaming because something she wanted had not been put out. Sometimes the thing she wanted was in fact on the table already but she had not seen it right in front of her. Then she complained about the food she had been given – too much or too little or something she felt sure she did not like. We did not want to put up with such behaviour. She acted like a thoroughly spoilt child, but in fact we did not give in to her and supply her every whim.

We began to tackle the problem by not paying too much attention to her bad behaviour. We had had no guidance about this but it seemed the only thing to do. If she fell off her chair we did not rush to pick her up but left her to pick up her chair and sit on it again. On occasion she actually injured herself by accidentally hitting her head on the radiator as she fell or by crashing into the cupboard, and we did attend to her then, but these mishaps were not too frequent. More space in the house might have helped the situation as she could have sat further away from other things.

If she did not want the food we gave her we did not replace it with something she preferred. If she said we had given her too much we told her to leave it. Her disappearing act also had to be dealt with and we found it best to refuse to allow her to return to the table if she ran away without permission. She did not accept this without a fight which continued month in, month out and gradually improved over the years. She had a minute appetite at the best of times, but to be deprived of the little that she had intended eating or, after running away, thought she might like to have eaten, did her little harm. I flatly refused to bother about the amount of food she ate. If she ate poorly at one meal she often made up for it at the next.

The food problem worried my mother-in-law, however. She is a wonderful person who has faced sorrow and difficulties in her own life and survived, but she is a born worrier. When Tanya sat in her baby chair one day and cried because her dinner was not in front of her, she said,

'Let me give her a crust to keep her going until dinner.'

'She won't eat her dinner,' I replied.

'Oh, of course she will. I often gave Leslie a crust to eat while I put the dinner out.'

She gave her the crust which Tanya ate hungrily. Then we sat down for the meal. Tanya refused to eat.

'Whatever is the matter with her?' asked mother-in-law.

'Well I did say she wouldn't be hungry if she ate the crust, didn't I?' I replied.

'A crust ought not to take her appetite away. If she were my child I'd be worried about her.'

On one occasion I remember speaking to my mother-in-law on the telephone while Tanya was staying with them for a few days. She related to me the happenings of the day, what time Tanya had woken up and what she had had to eat.

'She had a good breakfast of cereal, an egg and bread and butter. We had lunch about one, but she wouldn't eat much at all. I just don't know why she didn't want it.'

This did not surprise me in the least. After a 'good breakfast' around 8:30 in the morning Tanya would still be feeling quite full by lunch time. Having eaten much more breakfast than usual, with persuasion from grandma, she would be unable to do justice to lunch, however appealing it might be. Of course grandma had been used to feeding a hungry son who would eat everything put in front of him and ask for more. She now faced a little girl with a very small appetite which in contrast seemed abnormal and possibly even dangerous in her estimation. It did not worry me as I could see that she did not suffer as a result of her eating habits. At home she ate very little at each meal but often said that she felt hungry in between meals. I tried not to let her pick at food between mealtimes as, if she did, she could then eat even less at the next meal.

Quite by chance one day I met a family who had stopped their car to take their little girl to the swings. Grandmother and her daughter, who was expecting another child, began a conversation while the little girl and Tanya became friendly. Then grandma went to the car and fetched some biscuits and Ribena.

'Would your little girl like something to eat and drink?' she asked. 'My grand-daughter has such a poor appetite. She hardly eats anything at all. We get so worried about her when she just won't eat, so wherever we go we take something good for her to eat and drink. Whenever she will eat, we take the chance to feed her up. She won't eat anything when we get home for tea, you know.'

I declined her kind offer on Tanya's behalf and she proceeded to feed her grand-daughter. I wondered what would happen when mum produced the next baby and felt that they were laying the foundations for problems. Fortunately the child seemed quiet and well behaved. I considered suggesting that they should allow the child to miss a few meals until she felt hungry enough to eat with everyone else, but they were too busy feeding her and then said 'goodbye' and drove away.

Afterwards they often crossed my mind and I wondered if the food battle continued. When I met them the little girl had them just where she wanted them, being fed with good things whenever she mentioned that she would be prepared to eat. I felt glad that we had avoided that trap anyway, even if we had a lot of others from which to escape.

Dealing with tantrums

When Tanya could not get her own way (these conflicts often grew worse when we wanted to sit down and eat quietly) she would have a tantrum or just make as much difficulty for everyone as possible. The house in which we had lived in the Cotswolds had a small back porch with a door into it from the kitchen, another leading to the garden and a third into the toilet. We could lock the outer door and remove the key, she could not reach the latch on the toilet door and the inner door locked from the kitchen. When her behaviour deteriorated we gave her a warning:

'Behave yourself, or you will go outside.'

She knew what this meant. If this warning went unheeded, as it often did, we would take her and place her in the back porch and lock her in, saying,

'When you are quiet you can come out.'

She usually screamed loudly for several minutes but we took no notice. Within five minutes she had quietened down and a tearstained but sorry little girl was ready to be let out. This solved the immediate problem. If she caused further trouble we returned her to the porch. Over a period of time she visited the porch on many occasions and we did not see much improvement in her behaviour, but it proved to be a way of stopping the bad behaviour as it happened. However, after keeping this up consistently for a long time the threat of being put into the porch proved sufficient to stop her misbehaviour.

When we moved house we had no suitable back porch to use for cooling down, so we had to lock her outside the house instead. This worked equally well because she was older and could be put outside without coming to harm. We would put her outside the back door and say,

'We don't want you in the house with us if you behave like that.'

After running around the house screaming and hammering on the front and back doors, she would calm down and come in quietly when we unlocked the door. We did not find out what the neighbours thought and we did not go out of our way to explain. Perhaps they did not hear her above the sound of their television, but if they did hear they did not send for the NSPCC inspector.

Other people's opinions

We had found from experience that slapping Tanya had very little effect on her. She seemed totally unable to learn what she should not do by the usual method of a slap on the hand or across the legs, accompanied by a firm 'No'. We had tried to be strict with her from the time when she was tiny; it was not from lack of punishment that she misbehaved.

It therefore made us feel doubly upset when other parents made comments about the way we had brought her up and suggested that we spoiled her. We were struggling to cope with a difficult child and needed help and encouragement, not criticism. We were told that one mother kept her children away from Tanya because she gave them a bad example and we did not discipline her.

This made us think, however. When in public we tried to avoid a head-on confrontation with her. At home, could it be possible that we were not being as strict with her as we ought to be? If we stepped up the punishment perhaps she would respond; perhaps we had become too lax. So each time she did something she should not do, we made sure that she did not get away with it and we slapped her. At first she cried a little, but as we carried on with this strategy she began hardly to notice a slap and returned to the same behaviour which had provoked it. We tried this over a period of two weeks. Each time we slapped her she noticed it less. By the end of the two weeks I found that I had increased the slap to a hard smack and it had so little effect on her that it accomplished nothing positive at all. I did not want to begin battering my child so we resorted to the original treatment. If she became very destructive or aggressive the occasional slap then had some effect, but used too often, every time she did something of which we disapproved, the punishment became totally ineffective.

During the years when Tanya's problems were at their worst, we found it difficult to speak to other people about them. They had either come to their own conclusion that she had been thoroughly spoilt by us and was just a naughty girl who needed a good hiding, or they said when we tried to discuss the matter,

'You want to be thankful that you have a normal, strong and healthy child. There is nothing wrong with her.'

One person who, although not having voiced this sentiment, gave the impression that we were making excuses for something which was our fault, or imagining things which did not exist, agreed to care for Tanya for a couple of days during the school holidays. When I returned to collect Tanya she questioned me about her behaviour.

'Why is she always wanting something? She followed me into the kitchen and wanted a drink, then felt hungry. All day long she followed me around wanting something. Why is she like this? I give my child a pile of books to look at while I do my work and she stays there and looks at them. Is Tanya always given what she asks for?'

When people actually had her in their care for a while they began to see things they had not previously noticed. Had this friend kept her for a while longer she would have noticed that, despite the fact that she did not get everything she asked for, she still continued to ask, and ask, and ask!

We received a real slap in the face from one person. She began to talk to me about Tanya and vaguely mentioned that she did not know how to behave. I began to explain about her hyperactivity but she interrupted me by asking how long John had been with us and where he had lived before. When I said that he had been with us several years and had lived in a children's home for six months before that, she said,

'That accounts for it. He's such a good boy. He had good training at the Home before he came to live with you.' The conversation ended abruptly as I could think of nothing suitable to say in reply!

Changing moods

For much of the time Tanya was a cross, unhappy, miserable little girl. Yet in between she could be charming and a joy to be with. It always seemed that underneath the difficult behaviour lay the real Tanya trying to blossom but being constantly stifled by moods which swept over her uncontrollably.

On one occasion her change in mood was particularly noticeable. We went on a day's outing to the coast by train. The sun shone and all should have been well. We sat on the beach, ate our lunch and took Tanya to the baths where she enjoyed splashing around in the shallow pools with the other children. We met up with other people from the group with whom we had travelled and planned to walk along the promenade to see something further along the sea front. We all wanted to do this, except Tanya. She did not know what she wanted to do, but she definitely did *not* want to do what everyone else had in mind! Part of the way along the promenade an older couple caught up with us. As they came within earshot, Tanya ceased her moaning and complaining and dropped back to walk with them, a big smile on her face. They responded to her welcome and began to talk to her. She walked happily along with them chattering away and telling them all about herself, where she lived and how we had travelled to the coast. The couple reached their hotel and said 'Goodbye' to Tanya. The woman smiled at me and said,

'Such a sweet little girl. We did enjoy talking to her.' They began to cross the road to reach their hotel. As they moved out of earshot Tanya began moaning at the point where she had left off before the couple approached. They had been a sufficient distraction to take her mind completely off her problems.

We found over the years that distracting her often had more effect than punishing her. If we had a plan for each day, with meals at regular times and brief activities with plenty of variety, some problems could be prevented before they occurred. If we saw that a particular situation would be likely to cause trouble, the suggestion of doing something Tanya really liked instead, or the promise of something more interesting when we finished the present task, would remove the heat from the situation. We did not feel that this amounted to bribery, as it so easily could have done. A careful assessment of the situation and a plan of action made it possible to avoid the stress although, because of Tanya's swings in mood, this did not always guarantee success. We did try hard not to fall into the trap of saying,

'If you stop crying I will give you a sweet.'

Concentration

We had tried and tried with little success to interest Tanya in listening to stories, colouring or playing games. Her table in the living room had a box under it full of pencils, paints and colouring books. We encouraged her to sit here, but as soon as she had put the things on the table she fled to some other part of the house. Then one day, just before her fifth birthday, Tanya sat at her table and coloured in a picture for several minutes. The most she had managed previously was a minute.

In her bedroom she had a cupboard to house her dolls and other toys suitable for her age, and more books. When she took toys out of the cupboard to play with, everything fell onto the floor as she rummaged around for what she wanted. Having found the required toys she either left them on the floor or brought them downstairs and left them there.

The shed outside the back door housed her outdoor toys and we had purchased a swing set (two swings and a kind of swing boat) which we erected in the garden. It was a common occurrence for her to sit at her table in the living room for a few seconds, long enough to pull out all her books there, then dash upstairs and dig around in the bedroom, leaving it in chaos before charging downstairs and out of the back door to the swings, not settling at any one activity for more than a moment. After just a short time most of her toys would be scattered throughout the house and garden. I tried very hard to prevent this happening and encouraged her to help me tidy up, but on the whole I might as well have been talking to a brick wall. I had already lost her attention. This behaviour totally contradicted my plans for her. She did not allow us to share in activities which children normally enjoy with adult participation.

Prior to my marriage I lived near friends who had a little girl. She became a close companion of mine and at the age of three attended my wedding as flower girl. I had often taken her for a walk in the park to feed the 'gucks'. She chatted to me and we sang songs together when we went out for a ride in my car. She even came with me when I visited people in their homes and sat quietly while I talked to them for a short while. We shared so many things and loved to be together. Now I had my own little girl we were like strangers to one another. I longed to have a friendship with my own child which even slightly resembled the relationship I had shared with little Jenny. Instead I had constantly to think ahead to avoid trouble, cope with tantrums and clear up debris after she had passed by. I longed for the day when the little girl I dreamed of would emerge from the child who tore the house apart as she swept through it.

I often asked myself how one small child, in the space of a few minutes, managed to make a house look as if burglars had ransacked it. Over the years I learned to turn a blind eye to the mess and tidy up at the end of the day. It had always been my habit to clean up and then try to keep the house as tidy as possible until the next cleaning day. If I had kept to this method, or even tried to do so, it would have upset me to see the daily chaos around me. It became necessary to modify my methods and gradually encourage Tanya to keep things tidy and learn to tidy up after making a mess.

I remember that one day the daughter of a family friend called to see us. I had the washing machine on in the kitchen and had been washing clothes for about an hour. Tanya had by then become more imaginative in her play, but this involved making a huge mess. All her dolls and teddies were in the living room adjoining the kitchen and she had made 'camps' around the room with eiderdowns, blankets, and bedspreads draped over the chairs. As I worked all day it helped if the washing could be done at the weekend. The mess Tanya made while I did it seemed worthwhile if it meant I could get on with the work. When Iris arrived with her little son, I left the washing, asked her in and cleared a space for her to sit down amongst Tanya's playthings. Whether or not I mentioned the state of the room I cannot remember, but after she had gone I suddenly thought:

'Whatever must she have thought of the dreadful mess in this room?'

Some time later we visited her home and it made me very sure that she must have been amazed by the way we lived. Her home had beautiful furniture and carpets and not a thing

seemed to be out of place. Her son had a few toys visible but apart from these one would not have known that a child lived in the house. Although I had become accustomed to living in a mess that hardly ever disappeared completely, I still longed to tidy up and for the house to remain tidy for at least one day.

Diet

Prior to our marriage, both my husband and myself had chosen to follow a vegetarian diet. We therefore brought our children up the same way. We ate wholemeal bread which for a number of years I made myself. We limited the amount of sugar in our diet and ate honey in preference to jams and marmalade. Sticky cakes and puddings were not included in our diet as we preferred fresh fruit.

My mother wrote to me saying she had read somewhere that certain food and drink seemed to aggravate hyperactivity and one thing she noted was orange squash. We had not previously thought of our diet in relation to hyperactivity. Tanya had never been keen to drink fresh orange juice but always welcomed orange squash. We felt that anything which might help would be worth trying, whether or not we knew the reason why. We ceased to give her orange squash and within a short while noticed a difference in her behaviour. She seemed considerably quieter, but we reasoned that this might be our imagination. After a few days we gave her a glass of orange squash to see if it made any difference. Her reaction amazed us. She set off at tremendous speed and leaped around us. It took her about twelve hours to slow down to the level of activity she had reached minus the orange squash. So we banned it and tried to make sure that she did not have any when she went out somewhere without our supervision. My mother also mentioned that colourings in food could add to the hyperactive child's problems, so we began to read packets and tins to see what they contained, but we had no guidance from anyone regarding this and the orange squash remained the main thing we avoided.

5 School Days

The daily round
Each day we drove to school, which took us between twenty minutes and half an hour. For several years after she began school Tanya still sat in her car seat to travel. She would not sit still in the back seat so had to be tethered long after other children have no further need for car seats. I drove, with John sitting behind me and Tanya in her seat on the opposite side of the car. If Tanya lost her temper over something, she would fling anything within her reach at John. We were very glad of the car seat in such circumstances which were far too frequent for our liking. One day on the way to school, Tanya's mood was diabolical. I could not continue to drive with the commotion going on in the back seat. I stopped the car, took her out of her seat and said,

'See that field over there? I am going to put you into it. You can stay there all day and we will collect you on the way home. We will not put with such awful behaviour and we don't want you in this car.'

Her screams of anger turned into pleas for mercy. I had not expected it to work so effectively. She returned to the car much subdued and remained quiet for the rest of the journey. Probably it will be said that I should not have used such false threats on a child, but there comes a time when something drastic must be done.

After sitting in the car on the return journey both Tanya and John felt refreshed for an evening at home. As soon as they entered the house they both began wanting things. Tanya usually dashed into the house flinging her belongings in all directions. She ran at the settee, dived head first into it and stood on her head with her feet up the wall. Time and again I told her off about this but she never remembered. By this time of the day I felt at my lowest ebb. We had been up early in the morning, overcome the problems of dressing and eating breakfast, driven to school, and I had worked all day. After driving home, often to the accompaniment of disagreements in the back seat, all I wanted to do was sit down and relax for five minutes at least. I decided to go on strike to get this. I explained to the children how I felt and what I intended to do. When we entered the house I sat down with the post, slipped off my shoes and refused to do anything for at least five minutes. After a while Tanya realised that I would not even answer questions during that time. Having had that brief respite I could then make drinks for them, persuade Tanya to hang up her coat and put her shoes away, then begin to prepare a meal.

As Tanya grew older there were many things that she should have been able to do by herself. John had learned to dress himself before he started school, even if he had to be constantly told to hurry, or to put his sock on his foot instead of holding it in his hand. To this day, however, mornings are not Tanya's best time for coping. She always seems half asleep and things which can be done easily later in the day present big problems in the morning. At that time, not only would she not dress herself in the morning, but she did not want anyone else to help her either. She argued about her socks, moaned about her pants, did not want to wear a slip and found things wrong with her school uniform. All the while the clock crept on and tempers became frayed. The solution lay in taking her down for breakfast before she dressed, giving John time to dress quietly. She might still be disagreeing over the breakfast cereal or falling off her chair by the time he came downstairs fully dressed.

An older girl began taking a lift with us to school each day and usually arrived with time to spare. I brought Tanya's clothes downstairs and the girl helped a reluctant Tanya to dress each day while I tidied myself and the bedrooms before we left for school.

At the weekend, particularly on Sunday mornings, Tanya woke early. Often by seven o'clock the noise from the children's bedroom became so loud that we had to go in and try to quieten them, for fear of waking the neighbours up the road.

But on school days when she should be awake she never had much life in her.

During the day I was now working with mentally handicapped adults at a hospital near the children's school. I enjoyed this work very much and, although it demanded patience and physical strength because the patients were severely handicapped and some had severe behaviour problems, I felt able to relax whilst in that environment better than at home. This was probably because I need not become too involved and there were other people also engaged in caring for the same patients. At the end of the day I could leave the problems behind to be dealt with by someone else and the responsibility did not rest on me. My work became a rest for me and I could prepare myself to cope with Tanya in the evenings. Her problems were mine and no one else would take over if I found coping too difficult. At one time we thought that, had Tanya been our foster child instead of John, we might have asked for her to be placed elsewhere as we found her too difficult. Having produced her ourselves we were obliged to do the best we could under the circumstances.

Up to the age of about ten she needed constant attention at all times when awake. Her desire to pick up, move, empty or break things did not cease as it normally does with young children. She retained an irresistible urge to explore everything around the house. Many, many times we told her that she must not enter our bedroom without permission when we were in it or in another part of the house, but she still continued to go in when not watched. There she would examine bottles of perfume, try on creams and search through drawers. In the bathroom she climbed up to the shelves, removed caps from bottles, wasted toothpaste and tipped talcum powder everywhere. If left downstairs for a short while she opened drawers and cupboards or clambered onto the washing machine in order to see or reach things on the top shelf above it. Once she went into the kitchen and I heard her open the fridge and drop something. I hurried to see what she was doing. She had dropped a carton of eggs on the floor, smashing two of them, and had removed the top from a bottle of Ribena and spilt half of it on the eggs. To avoid this kind of disaster we were obliged to supervise her at all times.

As she grew older we noticed that her activities became less random. She tried to take perfume because she liked to smell nice and talcum power because she enjoyed playing with it, tipping it from container to container. She took tops off the bottles and spilt the contents because she had tried to make a drink and she moved books around because she took them to look at briefly and did not put them back where she had found them. Before I left her in any room I had to make sure that someone would look after her and call me if she began doing something dangerous or destructive. Her brother often had the job of keeping an eye on her while I fetched the washing in, or put the car in the garage. He would warn me if he thought something was amiss, but even so I often found that she had climbed up on something, certain that articles forbidden or delightful lay just out of sight and reach.

We had a large garden in which to sunbathe on warm days. It also needed to be cared for, or the car needed washing. At these times I found it easier to lock the back door and keep the key in my pocket than to try to keep an eye on her all the time. Invariably, if I wanted to be outside she would try to creep into the house and get into trouble while not observed. It became a way of life for all of us, but looking back on it, it now seems so strange. To have Tanya around the house was in some respects like having a mentally handicapped child; yet she appeared to be bright, intelligent, although unable to learn what we expected of her without a long and determined battle.

Clumsiness

Apart from finding her way into everything around the house and leaping about on the furniture, Tanya often acted like a bull in a china shop. She looked dainty and sweet but charged around bumping into objects and people, tripping over things and over her own feet and falling downstairs. We became very concerned about the latter as it happened too often. She always managed to make a good job of it – falling from top to bottom and almost knocking herself out. Fortunately she never managed to do herself any permanent damage.

On one occasion I woke early in the morning and found that both children were still asleep. I decided to take advantage of the respite to have a quick bath before Tanya awoke. Baths during

the day with Tanya around were a luxury I could not afford as it meant leaving her alone for a while. Before I had finished bathing I heard the bedroom door open. The next second a series of bangs and bumps and loud screams reached my ears. I grabbed a towel, leaped out of the bath and ran downstairs, dropping the towel as I went. Tanya lay in a heap at the bottom of the stairs, badly shaken but uninjured. Unknown to me, she had hidden a pair of my shoes in her room, walked out of the bedroom wearing them, caught her foot at the top of the stairs and fallen. She had been warned over and over again about this. I usually found hidden shoes and removed them, but this time she had hidden them well.

We found it a constant battle to ensure that things which could hurt her were kept locked away or hidden and that the house and garden were as safe as possible. There is a limit, however, to the number of accidents which can be avoided. Unless one has a purpose-built home, preferably a bungalow, with locks on all doors, windows and cupboards, accidents will continue to happen, however hard one tries. And even then it is impossible to eliminate every possible danger. Also, if the child does not learn the consequences of doing dangerous things, she will never learn to avoid danger or cope with potentially dangerous situations.

The Samaritans

Tanya responded best when we kept to a regular routine. Towards bedtime I would try not to overstimulate her. She would be asked to get ready for bed ahead of time and if the progress towards bed was fairly leisurely we managed to get her there with little fuss. When both children were in bed I would read each a story, as their tastes differed. John liked stories about trains and Tanya preferred very short stories with a picture to look at while I read. Problems arose if for some reason I had to be away at bedtime. The change of routine created by father putting her to bed unsettled her and, like most children, she tried him to the limit to see how far she could go before he became really cross. I always insisted that she remain in her room, even if she did not stay in bed. It worried Leslie if he heard her walking around the bedroom, opening and closing drawers for a long while after she had gone

to bed. He tended to return to the bedroom and insist that she get into bed and stay there, but this often had the effect of delaying her winding down towards sleep. With father downstairs she tried coming downstairs also, and once there began delving into everything as usual.

One evening, when Leslie had her in his care, she began to play him up. He tried to be very strict with her, to no avail. She repeatedly came downstairs and began racing around and being very cheeky. By the time I returned Leslie felt very worried by what had happened. She made him so annoyed by disobeying him that he became afraid of what he would do to her. He smacked her, but felt the urge to hit her really hard. Not having another adult around to talk to did not help him. When she continued to refuse to stay upstairs he admitted that he felt like picking her up and throwing her through the window. Instead, he went to the telephone and rang the Samaritans and told them the problem. It made all the difference having someone to talk to, and the crisis passed. We were later advised of the emergency telephone number for the Social Services department if we found ourselves with problems with which we felt unable to cope out of office hours.

As a result of this experience we visited the doctor and told him of the problems in general and Leslie's wish not to harm her. The doctor referred us to the paediatrician at the hospital. He wrote back to our doctor suggesting that jealousy of the foster children (we had had two other children for a brief time prior to John's arrival) contributed to her attention-seeking behaviour. He felt that it had been a behaviour problem right from the beginning and might need the help of a child psychiatrist. Because she had been born by vacuum extraction and was slow to breathe at birth he also wanted to find out more about her birth from the hospital where she had been born.

6   Help and Progress

Checking the details of Tanya's birth
The details of Tanya's birth corresponded with my memory of events. Her condition at birth was described as 'fair only'. Labour had lasted $13\frac{1}{4}$ hours according to the record (the actual time I know to be nearer $17\frac{1}{4}$ hours as I had been in labour for most of the night before going into hospital). By 2:30 in the afternoon the contractions were strong and by 3:50 I felt the urge to push, but did not fully dilate until 4:20. By 4:45 there had been little progress and everyone became concerned. The doctor decided to use vacuum extraction and applied the extractor at 4:55. Traction began at 5:05 and the baby's head was delivered at 5:10. At 5:14 the birth was complete. She was described as limp and apnoeic (not breathing). At 5:15 she gasped and at 5:22 cried. By 5:30 tone and colour were described as good. It had therefore been eight minutes that I lay after her birth, thinking that she must be still-born, until I heard her weak cry.

Visits to the child psychiatrist
We were referred to the psychiatrist when Tanya was about eight years old and he described her as 'typical of children with minimal brain injury'. He discussed a variety of games and occupations to help train co-ordination, spatial memory and fine skills and asked us to return at regular intervals to see how Tanya progressed. These visits proved very useful. I found it quite amazing that although I used similar methods every day in my work with mentally handicapped adults, I had been unable to think in terms of using them with my own child. I realised that I often expected too much from her, because she was normal, and when she could not concentrate on what I

wanted to do with her, gave up too easily. Instead, I needed to analyse what she could and could not do and begin by using large objects instead of expecting her to complete tasks which required fine movements and great concentration. He helped me to think of activities she could do and through them begin to develop other skills. Tanya enjoyed these visits as she liked the psychiatrist and it was a relief for me to be able to speak to someone who understood the problems we faced. He did not criticise us, but encouraged us to try out new ideas, some of which worked well and some which did not. If they were not viable he did not insist that they should be but suggested alternatives. He encouraged us to continue such activities as swimming and suggested that Tanya take up gymnastics and trampoline.

Swimming had always been very successful with Tanya. We first took her swimming when she was about nine months old. Before she could walk she wore arm bands and loved to 'dog paddle' around the pool without a care about the depth of the water. The exercise made her very sleepy so we had some peace and quiet for a while after swimming sessions. When she learned to walk she wanted to be in shallow water where her feet could touch the bottom and spent a lot of time running in and out of the pool, or under the hot shower. Eventually she learned to swim, but not until she went to swimming classes with her school and she had to face it as a lesson rather than a game.

We took up the suggestion of gymnastics. Tanya joined a group at the local Youth Centre. The group were all beginners of approximately the same age. The teacher proved to be quite an extraordinary person. He managed to teach the huge group of between 30 and 40 children single handed. Sometimes I stayed to watch. He had all the children under very strict discipline. When he called for silence a hush fell at once. This was excellent discipline for Tanya. He began and ended with all the children doing exercises together and in between they divided into small groups to practise different skills. I noticed that he called Tanya's name time after time:

'Tanya - no talking,' or 'On your tummy, Tanya,' or 'Tanya, arms, not legs,' and so on.

She often managed to face the wrong direction or do the

wrong exercise, but responded well to the classes and began to work as a member of a group. She did not complain about going but looked forward to sessions.

When we moved house she took up trampolining but this proved less successful than the gymnastics as it involved long waits for a turn on one of the trampolines. A gymnastic dance group formed and Tanya joined it with great enthusiasm. The running and leaping movements she had to perform used up a great deal of energy. Unfortunately the teacher moved away from the area and as another teacher could not be found the classes had to close after a couple of terms. She then joined the local Baptist Church's Girls' Club. There she enjoyed the variety of activities offered and proudly brought home things she had baked or made. Most weeks she wanted to attend but when the club reorganised to include boys she left, as she said that they were too rough and noisy.

Au pairs

We began having au pairs from Germany to stay with us before Tanya's birth. The first one to come, Marie-Luise, stayed for a year. Soon after her arrival I began to feel that it had been a mistake. Leslie had suggested that it would be a good idea as she could help me in the house after the baby's birth. In fact I ended up looking after her, which really did not help me at all! Looking back, I would not have missed the experience, and now that Marie-Luise is older and a mother herself, we are good friends. She thinks back on her youthful exploits and says,

'I must have been awful when I stayed with you.'

At the time she thought that we did not understand her and that we were sometimes being unkind to her. Her presence in our house had one main benefit. She prepared us for what Tanya would be like as she grew up. At the time we thought of her as a bit of a nuisance.

Every day after breakfast the floor needed sweeping as she dropped cereal everywhere. She resented being asked to clear it up herself but eventually agreed to do so. She never walked downstairs but leaped down three or four at a time and jumped into the hall, sending the rug skidding across the floor – and leaving it there. When she entered the sitting room she ran at the settee, leaped over the arm and crashed onto the seat, every time. When she walked through a room objects went flying and she seemed not to notice what had happened. Without our knowledge she bought candles to use in her bedroom – and one day set fire to her hair. I looked into her room one day and found that she had placed the electric fire on the bed, switched on, with clothes propped up in front of it to dry. When I warned her of the danger of doing this she retorted,

'It is quite all right. It is safe.'

I made sure that I looked into her room several times a day after that as we did not want to find ourselves homeless! She started to put up pictures all over the bedroom walls with sticky tape, damaging the new paint. When she washed her clothes she took over the sink for hours regardless of mealtimes and family routine, and when she did get around to cleaning her own room she began late in the evening and rearranged it completely – and noisily – after we had gone to bed. When we told her about these things, she either did not listen or became deeply hurt that we should be so unkind to her, not allowing her to do what she wanted. Because of her antics we felt too afraid to allow her to have much to do with Tanya as a small baby and as she made more work around the house than she cleared up, it was not exactly a successful year. As Tanya grew older people mistook her for Marie-Luise's baby as both were blonde haired and blue eyed and I am very dark.

Some years passed before we tried having au pairs again. It seemed to be a good idea to have someone to stay just for the summer months to care for the children during the holiday while I had to work. As Leslie worked on the estate adjoining our home he could keep an eye on the children and the girl had someone to call for in an emergency. This worked extremely well. We managed to find girls who were studying English and therefore needed to brush up their English conversation. The majority of girls we had to stay over several years were very capable. They loved cooking and housework and I found it difficult to stop them working, even when I arrived home.

'You sit down and have a rest, I'll get the tea ready. You must be very tired,' was the kind of greeting I received. Before the girls came from Germany I always made it quite clear that

Tanya required a lot of patience and needed amusing so that her brother could get on with his interests undisturbed. We did not want them to cook or clean the house, just to keep the children happy and safe while I worked. Despite this, I found that the house had been cleaned from top to bottom and all the meals prepared, particularly on those occasions when we had two girls staying, one on holiday and the other as au pair. I had to give in. Most of the girls found Tanya a problem and seemed to prefer to send the children out into the garden to play while they did the work. As we usually went away on holiday during the summer ourselves, the period when the au pair had to cope alone all day was not too long.

The girls often found it difficult to speak to the children and tell them what to do. It is one thing to learn English and another to be able to speak it well enough to give a child instructions or to tell him that his behaviour is not acceptable. One girl called Marita found that time and again Tanya would be in her room (which at other times of the year was our sitting room) nosing through her belongings or taking her leather boots out into the garden and wearing them. She disliked telling Tanya off about this as she either ignored her or had a screaming fit with which Marita found she could not cope. The most I could do was find out what had happened during the day, make it as plain as possible to Tanya that she must not disobey Marita and ask Marita to reinforce the rules during the day.

We ceased having girls from Germany during the summer about two years ago. The last girl found it very difficult to cope with the children. She told me that all day long they argued with each other or pestered her. I asked her to take them out to the nearby park at least once a day to play ball games and generally let off steam. However, Tanya refused to go out unless they were going to the shops to buy sweets and the German girl's English did not allow her to insist that they went out, but *not* to the shops. I asked her to occupy Tanya in one part of the house if they did not go out, thus allowing John to pursue his interests of reading and stamp collecting in peace. She failed to make this work either, and suggested that Tanya needed children of her own age to play with during the day. This would have been ideal, but one cannot provide playmates for one's children out of the blue. Tanya had an on-off relationship with two girls of her age living nearby. They tended to play with each other and leave Tanya out of their plans. During the summer they both went away on family holidays or to stay with grandparents. If at home they were allowed to roam further afield than I would let Tanya go without adult supervision.

The answer that we came up with was to leave Tanya with married students and their families at a local college. The students live in blocks of flats surrounded by an enormous garden. During the holiday we now pay one family to be responsible for her but she has the opportunity to play with any other babies and children living in the flats. Tanya is very fond of babies and enjoys helping the mothers to care for their babies or toddlers. All the students make the best use of the warm weather and almost live outside when the sun shines. Caring for the younger children has helped Tanya to develop responsibility. She also observes their temper tantrums and any babyish behaviour and likes to discuss with me what certain children have been doing, what she felt was wrong with their behaviour and what should have been done about it. The fresh air, the room to run around, people to meet, young children to care for and older ones to play with, have all helped her to grow up and become more mature. We were very glad to have the German girls with us when the children were young, but from about ten years of age the more stimulating environment has been the best answer.

Education

Tanya began school at the age of four-and-a-half and attended mornings only until she reached five. She settled into school reasonably well and only once or twice refused to be left there. I overcame this by walking into the school with her and seeing her into her classroom where she happily settled down at once with the other children. I did not receive urgent messages from the teacher complaining about her behaviour so concluded that they were coping. On the first report the teacher noted, 'Tanya's conduct could be improved.' I asked the former headmistress recently what she remembers of Tanya when she began school.

'She was a child who never kept still. She reminded me so much of my own son when he was small – always racing around and never stopping,' she said.

They had trouble with her in this respect during the years that followed. During assembly and story time this showed up most of all. The teacher found it impossible to read to the group if she did not have Tanya sitting with her. If she allowed Tanya to sit with the group she quickly lost interest, distracted the other children or wandered off to find something which interested her more. During assembly her class teacher found it easier to sit Tanya on her knee or beside her. She did not want to pay her special attention but it seemed the best way to keep the peace. If left to sit with the other children, problems developed. This continued for several years. One teacher commented to me,

'All the children in the school will be sitting listening to a speaker. If a disturbance occurs, it is guaranteed that Tanya will be causing it.'

This had an adverse effect on Tanya in that other children labelled her as a trouble maker. When they wanted to hear something or listen to an interesting story, she would be there upsetting the situation. This built up resentment against her over the years and she found that children refused to play with her. If they played team games, they did not choose her. This in turn made her angry and spiteful towards them. The worst retaliation she tried occurred when a group of children and teachers were standing around a bonfire. For no apparent reason she pushed one of the boys towards the fire. Fortunately a teacher caught him or he would have fallen face down in the fire and been severely burned.

Throughout Tanya's school reports comments are made regarding her restlessness. At six years old her report read:

Conduct variable. Tendency to be over-talkative and to lack concentration, yet responds positively to correction. Tanya is willing to please and though she finds some difficulty in sitting still and persevering she nevertheless displays a helpful and generous nature.

By the time Tanya reached seven she still lacked concentration:

A noticeable improvement in conduct which we hope will continue. Tanya is making progress but much more could be made but for lack of concentration.

Things seemed more hopeful by eight years of age:

Tanya has developed a better attitude to work now her skills are improving. Although Tanya is a slow developer, improvement can be seen in her work. Praise and insistence on good work is proving well worth while.

'It is pleasing to see how much Tanya has matured this year,' stated the report the following year. One of the teachers commented: 'When she settles down Tanya works well, but she is easily distracted.' Later the same year we read:

Tanya shows a growing keenness to do well and is happier as a result. She is beginning to relate better to other children than she has previously.

Another comment on the same report said, 'School work is not the most important thing to Tanya but she is beginning to apply herself.' Aged ten her report reads:

Tanya is showing signs of caring about her work. She is more enthusiastic now and sometimes even takes the initiative in choosing her own subject. Tanya has some good points and with encouragement I am sure that she will achieve a measure of success.

During a parents' evening Tanya's teacher said, 'I find that I have to be very strict with her. I noticed her one day in particular. She had work to do on her desk. A few minutes later I looked to see if she was working. Her desk was empty. She had moved to another desk, but as she had settled down and appeared to be working, I left her there. Next time I looked, she had moved again, but seemed busy, so I let her continue. When she moved yet again I realised that she should not be allowed to shift around like that even if she appeared busy in between moves. Why should she get away with things that the other children would not be allowed to do?'

Tanya consistently found difficulty in maths and needed a great deal of assistance from the teacher. Her reports read,

'Appears to have difficulty understanding mathematical concepts.' 'Slow to grasp new concepts.' 'Still confused by basic number concepts.'

Her reading likewise hit problems. The teacher at the time remembers that she found it very difficult to teach her:

'I tried all ways to help her to read. I had just about given up hope of her ever learning to read when she suddenly grasped the idea and was away.'

Physical education brought the comment:

'Light and quick on her feet. Expresses herself well in music and drama. Dislikes team work, not always alert.' When swimming lessons began the teacher noted that she had plenty of confidence and made excellent progress.

The bright spot in Tanya's school life has always been music. Soon after she began school her ability to sing was noticed. She led the infants through their songs in the annual school concert and soon had a solo spot each year. She began to learn the recorder at about eight years of age and made a fairly good start. She joined the choir and enjoyed this very much.

'Singing very good, excellent timing,' appeared on her report.

A year later her recorder playing had improved considerably.

Tanya is most enthusiastic and keen to do well. Her playing is beautifully controlled now and has a sweet tone. Her responses are quicker in class. I am very pleased. Well done.

Tanya's school days have been far from easy. She has experienced difficulties in fitting into expected patterns of behaviour. Conforming to other people's ways is not easy for a child who is finding difficulty in disciplining herself. It helped Tanya being in a school with small classes. The whole school is small enough to create a family atmosphere. The emphasis placed on music has helped Tanya to develop and feel that she is a success in at least one area. The headmaster's enthusiasm for swimming and his ability to teach the children and prepare them for swimming certificates has been another area in which she could do well. In addition to the regular school curriculum, the pupils are offered private lessons in piano and prose and verse. Her progress with the piano has been slow but she is now making progress. Speech lessons provide an outlet for the actress within her. When she tried her first examination in speech her chances of success seemed slim as she did not try very hard and disliked practising the pieces. However, on the day, she summoned up all her powers and came away with the second highest marks received by the children from the two schools at the examination centre.

A definite improvement

By the time Tanya reached ten years of age we began to see a marked improvement in her behaviour at home. We had moved to our present home when she was still nine years old and at that time felt it necessary to explain to our neighbours that we had problems.

'If you hear screams and the doors being banged, please don't be worried,' I told them.

This did happen on quite a number of occasions but in a few months we noticed that Tanya actually began to listen when we reprimanded her, instead of flying into a frenzy which lasted a long while. She seemed to be taking control of the situation rather than circumstances controlling her. We began to see more and more of the beautiful, cheerful and happy Tanya who had so often been buried by the waves of difficult behaviour which swept over her. Between ten and eleven years of age the speed with which she moved slowed down and accidents grew less and less. We did spend some hours in casualty one evening after a bad fall when she had been confined to the house on a very wet day, but this was an exception.

Putting on the pressure

Now that Tanya showed an improvement we felt that the time had arrived really to put on the pressure to eliminate the behaviour problems she still demonstrated, before she should begin to experience teenage problems. Keeping her bedroom tidy had always proved too big a task for Tanya. She never succeeded in extracting one item from her wardrobe without half a dozen things following it. The removal of one book from the book case always caused an avalanche. When she tried to tidy up, things just got into a worse state and she would have a fit of temper and refuse to persevere. Chaos reigned in her

room – but at least we now had it confined to her room and the rest of the house escaped the worst of the problem. I decided to reward her for keeping her bedroom tidy. We agreed on 50 pence a week pocket money in return for a tidy room. We began by clearing the room up and putting everything in place. Tanya did little to help in the initial stage. If she managed to keep the room tidy from Sunday until Thursday she could have her 50 pence. If the room deteriorated during these days the pocket money diminished accordingly. Some weeks she managed to claim the whole 50 pence, other weeks she did not fare so well. One week she received money from another source. Her bedroom deteriorated at once.

'I don't need to keep my bedroom tidy this week,' she announced. 'I already have money for this week.' We had to watch this and make sure that gifts of money were controlled.

The weeks when Tanya received reduced pocket money taught her a lesson. If she made an awful mess in the room, rather than lose money, she learned to tidy her room up again before Thursday arrived. At first this involved pushing clothes and dolls under her bed but this gradually improved when told that this did not constitute 'tidying up' or qualify for 50 pence. She gradually developed the patience to sort things and place them in the correct drawers and cupboards or to hang them up. We have now progressed to the stage where she is able to tidy her room completely unaided and make a good job of it. It is rewarding for us to walk into her room and see her happy smiling face and listen to her singing as she carefully removes all the things on her dressing table, sorts and dusts them and returns them to the clean surface. She carefully lines up her shoes on one side of the room, keeps her toys in the cupboard and is able to use her record player as it is no longer covered in piles of rubbish. She loves the praise she receives and likes to stand back and admire her tidy room.

Internal troubles

Tanya's health has always been reasonably good. She had the usual childhood illnesses but avoided any complications. She has always tended to look pale except after exercise in the fresh air. Over the years, however, she has suffered from stomach pains. These suddenly appeared, lasted on and off for several days and disappeared again. Just before she reached her eleventh birthday she had a bout of these pains and we visited the doctor. By the time we had an appointment they had gone again so he asked us to return when they recurred. We were unable to make an appointment which 'coincided with the pains, however. Since her eleventh birthday these pains have diminished, having built up over the years until then.

Occasionally Tanya gets mild eczema on the back of her legs, particularly during the summer, and it is then irritated by the chlorine in the water at the swimming pool. She has had this on and off since babyhood. We did not consider any connection between either the stomach pains or eczema and hyperactivity until fairly recently. Having met other mothers of hyperactive children I now find that many of them have experienced similar additional problems. Some suffer from hay fever, asthma, stomach pains, headaches and so on, which have disappeared when the hyperactivity has been dealt with successfully.

Remembering the old self
One day recently Tanya came and put her arms around me and said,

'Mummy, what was I really like when I was little? I must have been awful.'

We talked about the things she used to get up to, some of which she remembered but many of which she had forgotten. We are so happy to have a new Tanya around that we do not want to remember her old self too often. In fact it seems like someone's else's story as it fades into the past. We spend a great deal of time together talking and sharing ideas. She asks searching questions and discusses other people's problems in a very mature way. She is now very demonstrative, flinging her arms around me and saying,

'Mummy, I do love you so much. I don't know what I would do without you.'

Since Tanya moved into the senior section of her school, her improvement has been accelerated. Physically she has developed little, for which I am glad. She needs time to mature mentally before she has the added problems of becoming a young woman. She has grown a little taller and takes a pride in her appearance. She is interested in writing letters, spends time by herself making things, colouring or painting. Cookery interests her and she listens with interest to cookery courses on television and experiments for herself. Offers of help now come my way and recently Tanya and her brother actually managed to clean the car together. John supervised and Tanya did most of the work, as she wanted to learn how to do it properly. They are able to sit together in the same room and watch a television programme or enjoy a conversation without Tanya stirring up trouble.

A few weeks ago Tanya did something which she should not have done. I asked her to stop and she became very annoyed and argumentative. She went away in a bad mood whispering threats. A little later as she sat in the car with me, she put her arms around my neck and said,

'I am sorry, mummy. I got confused about what I should have been doing. You were quite right and I should have taken notice of you. I'm sorry.'

Those words were perhaps the most beautiful I have heard her say. They represent so much progress and a pulling together rather than a pulling apart, which used to occupy so much of our time. But the most special moment is when she wraps her arms around me and says,

'Mummy, I do love you.'

Peace at last

It is wonderful to share at last that close relationship with Tanya which I had sought from the first. It is possible, now that she can be still, and she delights in it as much as I do. Now I have to face the problem of letting her go, little by little. Because we have gone through so many problems and she has needed so much protection in order to survive, I have difficulty now in really believing that she can cope with things by herself. In order to overcome this it has been necessary very gradually to allow her a little more freedom. As she proves that she is able to cope then I am able to allow her more freedom. This is really for my benefit as I cannot face up to her growing up and not needing to be observed all day. At first she began to go out to play nearby and by now is able to ride her bicycle to the local shops to fetch the paper. She preferred to attend church with her friends with whom she goes to school, rather than with the family. This has worked very well and she is always at the right place at the right time to be collected after the services. Sometimes she goes home to tea with a friend from school. When we visit the town, she likes to visit certain shops and arrange to meet me later. All these things have happened gradually so that I can learn to let go.

'Please can I go with the school on holiday this year, mummy?' she asked a few weeks ago.

The teachers are very happy to include her now, although they had reservations a couple of years ago. That year I went with the school to care for several of the girls, including Tanya. Now she is too old to need mum to go with her, but I feel weak at the thought of waving goodbye to her for a week. If Tanya is patient with me, I hope to improve in this respect as the years go by!

The headmaster remarked recently that the school is small enough to have a family atmosphere and that this is good in many ways. However it is small enough for everyone to know each other very well and to remember past events clearly, which is not always advantageous. He felt that the children remember the old Tanya and they, like me, need time to adjust to the new, more responsible and mature Tanya. They sometimes treat her in the way she deserved when really annoying everyone in sight. She has stopped doing these things, but they have not fully realised that she has changed.

A new chapter lies just ahead. She will soon begin to attend a different school, one of the local comprehensives. She will be an unknown quantity to the other children. It will be very interesting to see how she will get on in a new environment. It will also be a new stage in my learning to let her go, as she makes her way to and from school and becomes involved in various school activities. Time will tell how well we are both able to adjust in this new situation.

PART TWO

Comparing Experiences

Introduction

During the years when my daughter's hyperactivity caused the most problems I had no contact with parents of other children who were struggling with similar difficulties. Recently I began to meet more and more parents whose accumulated experiences are important evidence in any discussion of the causes, symptoms and nature of hyperactivity – quite apart from the light they shed on what it means to have to cope with a hyperactive child. They often express a great sense of loneliness and frustration, and from my own experience I know just how they feel. Without meeting others in similar circumstances there is a tendency to think that the child's problems are unique. Even now, with my daughter's problems resolved, it is extremely interesting for me to hear other parents' views and to notice the similarities and differences in experiences. Had I known others with whom to share views and ideas a few years ago, it would have helped tremendously. Whether you are a parent experiencing problems, or a relative, friend, teacher or member of the medical profession involved with such a child, I am sure that you will benefit from these insights into the lives of such families.

From where other people stand, a hyperactive child often appears to be very disobedient and thoroughly spoilt by his parents. Friends and even relatives may gradually withdraw because they do not understand the situation and value their property too much to allow an undisciplined child into their home. From a safe distance they may say,

'If that were my child, I'd give him a good hiding. They are too soft with him.'

The parents then have the double burden of a difficult child and the rejection of those people whom they might expect to show understanding or receive help from in some way. Even their doctor may not understand the problem they face and be unable to give any useful advice. The Hyperactive Children's Support Group helps to restore confidence to parents as they meet and share experiences (see p. 175). Most of all, the Group provides a practical method for helping children through the use of a food programme.

As I interviewed parents I found a wide variety of problems and yet a great many similarities. 'Hyperactivity' is not always an apt term to use to describe the children, as some may be less active, yet in other respects show similarities to the very definitely hyperactive children. The term 'hypoactive' is given to some children who lack motivation yet may show many of the characteristics of children termed 'hyperactive'. Other children swing between overactivity and underactivity. You will notice the range of behaviour in the descriptions of the various children. Some children whose families I contacted are extremely difficult but have never been called hyperactive. This is either because they are now older and grew up at a time prior to the use of the term or because their particular medical adviser prefers not to label children as hyperactive, or does not recognise the condition (see p. 184).

There are a wide range of symptoms which include restlessness, irritability, excessive crying, temper tantrums, short attention span, destructiveness, poor sleep patterns, speech problems, low frustration tolerance, poor peer relations, proneness to accidents, insensitivity to pain, poor bladder control, and so on. Some children exhibit many of these symptoms. For some the problems of temperament are worse and for others the lack of sleep or overactivity is the main difficulty. In fact, two children with problems of this kind may appear quite different from one another as they have different symptoms within the range of symptoms.

It is interesting to notice that of the mothers who mention pregnancy and birth a number had problems. These include a tendency to miscarry, long labour, use of forceps or vacuum extractor, and some seem wary of the use of Pethidine as a result of their experiences.

7 An Unsolved Problem

First I would like to look at five children whose parents have not found a lasting solution to their problems. Simon's mother has had some contact with the Hyperactive Children's Support Group; William and Rodney's parents are learning to cope with the situations as they arise. These boys are not yet teenagers and their parents are concerned for the future. Brian is just entering the world of work and Philip is an adult whose family suffered because of his problems when he was young.

Simon
There are three children in Simon's family. He is four years old, his sister is three and another brother is not yet two. His mother finds great difficulty in communicating with him. She has to approach him and look him in the face before he will listen to her and she can obtain a response. His parents began to wonder if he had a hearing problem, so he had some hearing tests. These were not conclusive because of his age at the time. His mother finds that the more freedom he is given, the more liberties he takes. She finds that he responds best to strict consistency from her.

Simon and his sister are allowed to play at the front of the house so that they may ride their bikes and cars on the pavement. It is a very safe area as their house is situated in a cul-de-sac. However, an irate neighbour came to the house one day saying,

'I'm going to knock your child over one day! He just ran into the road in front of my car and held his hands up to stop me. He just stood in the path of the car and expected me to stop. He has done this before. One day I may not see him. Please don't let him out.'

Simon does not get on well with his brother and sister, nor with the children at the play group he attends. At home he fights and bites his younger brother and sister and he has bitten other children at the play group too. Because he is small for his age he gets teased and he responds with a high pitched scream which encourages other children to tease him again to get the same response.

Lack of sleep has not been a problem with Simon, although whenever he is awake in his bedroom he gets up to destructive activities. He likes books but cannot look at them without ripping them. He attacks his bedclothes, too. One day he removed all the covers and made holes in the mattress. Fitted sheets were the answer to this problem. At one time his mother was forced to keep all his clothes downstairs as he made such a mess in his room by pulling everything onto the floor. Now the solution is to turn his chest of drawers to the wall to prevent him opening the drawers.

Crayons had to be banned from the house as Simon took them and dragged them over surfaces and walls. His mother is envious of friends whose children will sit and colour pictures in books rather than misuse the crayons. Instead, Simon and his mother go for long walks with the two younger children to keep him occupied. Grandma prefers them not to visit her at home as she has china on display, and china and Simon do not go together. Instead she visits their home.

Inside the house Simon's mother finds it easiest to confine the children to the two downstairs rooms by keeping the door to the hall locked and a baby gate across the kitchen door. This prevents Simon from getting up to mischief while she is cooking or dealing with the other children. Until recently it proved unsafe to allow Simon into the enclosed back garden by himself as he would find something dangerous or destructive to do instead of playing with his toys, although his baby brother could safely be left to run around without coming to any harm.

The family have received support from the Health Visitor. Simon also had an assessment from a paediatrician and saw a speech therapist, since his speech has not developed very well. He does not ask questions as children normally do but is limited to 'Why?' The speech therapist found that he had a comprehension level of 5 years. He is, however, only just learning to understand what he is told. For instance, when out shopping, he runs away and steals sweets and cannot understand that this is unacceptable. His father began leaving him at home and taking his sister shopping instead. He pleaded to be taken too, so his mother carefully explained that he could not go because he took sweets. The following week he surprised them by asking,

'Next time daddy goes shopping, can I go? I won't take sweets.' His mother rejoiced that they actually seemed to be getting through to him.

Simon's mother finds that she cannot meet friends and have a chat because she always needs to watch Simon, so she feels starved of conversation. Despite the difficulties she has with him she feels sympathy for him as she thinks back over her own childhood. She remembers that she herself was not always an angel, that she, too, was guilty of some awful crimes: such as taking her mother's washing-up liquid and using it all to draw patterns on the pavement, and pinching babies in their prams outside shops to make them cry. When their mothers returned she would be rocking them and so would be congratulated on quietening them.

'Once I broke into a friend's house, taking my little sister with me. I knew the friend had some sweets and my mother had forbidden me to have any for some reason. I must have caused my mother an awful lot of problems and heartbreak,' she confides.

Since infancy Simon has had occasional outbreaks of cold sores and eczema. Once his chin became raw and then covered in pus. He had to go into hospital for ten days on this occasion. He seemed quite well behaved whilst there, but later his mother found that he had received drugs to keep him quiet. At the time the chin problem was thought to be impetigo but recently the doctor has decided that the recurring problem is possibly herpes.

Although much of his behaviour is similar to children who are regarded as hyperactive, his mother does not like to think of him in this way. His behaviour problem is worse than his overactivity. His grandmother also insists that his mother's behaviour when young, although very difficult, could not be called hyperactive. Simon seems so similar to his mother in a number of ways and she prefers to think of him as experiencing a number of problems which cause great difficulty within the family rather than labelling him 'hyperactive'. Although she has had contact with the Hyperactive Children's Support Group, she is not fully convinced that the Feingold Food Programme recommended by them is helpful in Simon's case. She tried it for a while, but not fully. She makes sure now that his diet is good and that he eats brown bread. His behaviour still causes many problems which they are learning to live with rather than trying to solve.

William

Cynthia has two children. Her elder son presented no unusual problems, but her second son has been quite different.

'Had he been my first child, there would have been no more,' she states firmly.

His mother has had four pregnancies. The first and third resulted in a miscarriage. There are two and a half years between the two boys.

William's uncontrollable thirst has been one of the greatest causes of anxiety within the household. This is a problem which is not uncommon amongst hyperactive children. His thirst became noticeable from birth; when he had a feed he would drink 14 or 16 ounces of milk, rather than the few usually consumed by new born babies. I met him briefly as a toddler; he ran around the house carrying his cup with him, and as soon as it was empty he returned to his mother for more, all day long. Cynthia remembers getting through 30 nappies a day, as he needed changing so frequently. She says that drinks and nappies dominated her life during his early years. She vividly remembers the summer of 1976 when Britain experienced a drought. At the time William was two-and-a-half years old. She would lie in bed at night with feelings of panic sweeping over her, as the local reservoir had only enough water left to last for two-and-a-half weeks. Visions of no water to give William and no water to wash the nappies became a nightmare for her. Fortunately rain fell before the reservoir ran dry!

I met William and his mother Cynthia again recently and

enquired about his thirst and his general development since we last met. His continual requests for drinks have caused many an argument over the years, it seems, and his behaviour brings his parents a great deal of worry. Until he reached two years of age he would wake as many as 12 times every night. He began to sleep through the night when his father changed his job and needed the spare room as an office. The two boys shared the same room from then on, which altered his sleep pattern. Now he is older, he goes to bed about eight in the evening but is wide awake by six. Cynthia insists that he stays in bed until 6:30 each day. At that time, one parent turns on the gas fire for him and leaves him to eat his breakfast whilst he watches Breakfast TV and exercises with the 'Green Goddess'. By 7:15 he is ready for school. His mother leaves for work at eight and his father has to watch him carefully to make sure he does not slip out of the house before 8:30, or he would arrive at school before anyone else and be knocking at his friends' doors almost before they were out of bed!

Educationally there have been difficulties. At four years old he began play school, but did not settle. At five he began school and liked it. Cynthia receives complaints about him, however. He has little concentration, she is told, and he keeps moving around the classroom. His teacher cannot understand how two children from the same household can be so different. Big brother has always been so easy to deal with and is a very good student with top marks in everything. Not so little brother. Now that he is nine years old he has many friends at school, but he always likes to be the leader.

William lives mainly out of doors, even when it is pouring with rain. This causes his parents a great deal of concern as he disappears regularly, but they try not to worry as they know that he is with his friends at any one of a dozen or so houses in the area. At least, they always hope that he is with his friends. His parents find him very difficult to control. In an effort to use up some of his energy the family often go swimming together.

His grandparents are very good with William. They recognise that he is a difficult child but do not blame his parents for these problems. Everyone notices that he has improved as he has grown older. His mother says of him,

'He is a very lovable child and it is easy to forgive him. It does concern me regarding his future. I just wonder what he will be like as a teenager and an adult.'

Rodney

This young man is nearly eleven years old and has a sister aged twelve. He is small for his age but is a very good looking boy, with an attractive personality. His attractiveness can wear thin after a while as he seems overpowering, particularly when confined to a small space such as a car. He is rarely to be found at home. After school he changes his clothes, gets his bike out of the shed and is gone. If not riding, he is walking or running and may be miles away from home in a very short time. This causes his mother great concern at times. When younger he would be missing for hours, sometimes not returning for meals. It is not easy to find one small boy who might be anywhere, in any direction, in a town which has many parks and play areas. Fortunately he has come to no harm, although it is a cause for concern. On one occasion a stranger knocked at the door asking if Rodney might join a local children's football team. He had observed him playing on a pitch at least two miles from home and had spotted his talent. His family were not aware that he played on that pitch.

I asked Rodney's mother when he first developed problems. She told me that he seemed good as a baby; it was his sister, Laura, who proved difficult, did not sleep well and later got into all kinds of mischief. She quickly grew up into a caring, motherly little person, however. When Rodney reached the toddler stage his activity became non-stop. He began to sleep less, not going to sleep until late at night and waking with his sister, also an early riser, at five in the morning. The children shared a bedroom and kept each other occupied to a certain extent. However the nights gradually became one long play session and Laura needed more sleep. She moved into a room of her own. Rodney missed her company and became destructive, stripping the wallpaper off the walls, ripping and damaging things. He did not seem able to find enough to keep himself occupied and so resorted to spoiling things, his mother thinks.

In addition to hyperactivity, Rodney has another problem.

His mother thinks that he was about ten months old at the time when it first developed. He whimpered a lot one night when they were away on holiday, and felt sweaty to her touch when she went to check him. In the morning she found difficulty in rousing him. As a nurse she suspected hypoglycemia (there is a history of diabetes in the family). She fed him with sweet food and took him to the doctor. He wrote to her own doctor, but he did not agree with the diagnosis. Six months later the problem arose again, but in the morning Rodney lay motionless. His father thought he had died as he could not rouse him. They rushed him to hospital and hypoglycemia was confirmed. He has not become a true diabetic, his mother says, but he seems to use up so much energy that he occasionally reaches the point where it cannot be replaced. When he began school he would become hungry during the night and would go downstairs, take food out of the cupboards and turn the cooker on. Once up, he would then go to his sister's room and pull all the bedclothes off her bed. All the handles on the doors had to be changed to prevent his night wanderings and his mother found that she had to give him food near his bedtime in order to prevent his night-time hunger. He has an early breakfast, too, as he uses up so much energy every day that his food is very important.

The hypoglycemia has sent him into hospital a number of times. Once, when he felt ill, he fell asleep on the pavement on his way home from school. In the hospital they have never observed his hyperactivity, perhaps because he is taken in only when at a low ebb following a recurrence of the hypoglycemia, or perhaps because he is in a strange environment. He tends to lie around and sleep for long periods in the hospital.

I am told that this is not an isolated case, and that a number of children are both hyperactive and hypoglycemic.

Rodney has had considerable problems with his education. His behaviour at school is often disruptive. His parents moved him to a private school for a while, thinking that the smaller classes might help him, but he still experienced difficulties and did not learn to read. Instead he began to pretend to read by making up the words as he went along, convincing anyone not actually looking at the book that he could read the words printed. He is confused by the letters 'p' and 'b', and when he becomes excited about something that he wants to write down his writing becomes illegible. The local educational psychologist saw Rodney and assured his parents that he is in fact a very able person. He suggested another primary school in the area where there is a great emphasis on sport, which he felt would act as a reward for Rodney. In this school he still does better in a smaller group and when put in the larger class is not able to cope so well. His new teacher said to his parents during his first week at the school, 'I thought that I would not survive having Rodney in my class.' She now sees that he is eager to please other people and she finds him full of fun, but realises that he needs a very firm hand if he is to accomplish anything.

'But he is not up to the standard of the other children in his class,' said his parents.

'Don't worry,' replied his teacher. 'With the personality that he has, he is going to be a success in life.'

When he was about nine years old his mother suggested that he ought to get down to some work at school, or he would not be able to find a job when he left school.

'Don't worry, mum. In ten years' time there won't be any jobs – everyone will be on the dole,' he reasoned!

Sport now takes up a great deal of Rodney's time in and out of school. He is as keen as ever on football and is able to play tennis and badminton with adults, and win, although he has had no coaching in these. A gymnast visited his parents to ask permission to coach him, as he has natural ability and he felt that Rodney would be able to compete nationally. Rodney showed no interest, however, as he did not want to work consistently.

Rodney's parents are concerned for his future. He moves soon to a secondary school and although he reads reasonably well now, they wonder how he will get on. There have been so many problems in the past that they naturally worry about what the future holds for this butterfly of a boy.

Brian
From infancy until the time that Brian went to junior school, he rose very early in the morning. As soon as he awoke he would begin ransacking cupboards and drawers, causing his mother so many problems that eventually almost everything

had to be locked away or kept out of reach. He had a stack of toys in his bedroom but preferred to chew the sheets.

Brian had tremendous energy and bounce, his mother remembers. In fine weather this could be expended in outdoor games, but at other times it resulted in his jumping on and off the chairs if confined to the house. His mother did not consider this to be too unusual but it did worry her that he seemed to have a higher than average number of accidents, in spite of the extreme care taken to keep dangerous equipment out of his way. They made many trips to the hospital as a result of these mishaps.

Attendance at a play group run by a former teacher gave his parents some relief, but after a while his mother was asked to reduce his days of attendance from three to two. Another play group in a large hall then took him for the one day and the larger space seemed to use up more of his energy. At four years of age he began a nursery school run by nuns, who saw him as 'quite a handful' but thought him 'a darling boy'. They even offered to have him during the school holidays, too, when his mother took a part-time job. His mother thought that perhaps they took him as a form of penance!

On progressing to infant school he began to earn reports of distractibility, lack of concentration, unfinished work and careless behaviour and although, as he grew older, he had bouts of enthusiasm and good results, much of his behaviour seemed bad and silly and he became the class buffoon. This continued throughout his school career, his mother recalls, and he needed extra tuition out of school hours to give him a basic grounding in English, maths, biology and art.

At 16 Brian left school with one CSE grade 1, several lower grades and two failed GCE 'O' levels. The local college came to his rescue with a City and Guilds course in catering. He worked quite hard at this mainly practical course and also retook two 'O' level subjects, which he passed. Another college then accepted him for an hotel catering and house-keeping course. He found this much harder and needed considerable prompting from his parents to do the set work. He managed to obtain the diploma, however, and has been accepted as a trainee manager for a chain of hotels. This will mean that he will live away from home. His mother feels that

this will give him a chance to find out whether he can discipline himself.

Brian's mother mentioned to me that temperamentally her husband is subject to tremendous swings of mood, attempting far more activities than he can cope with adequately, and so succeeding at only a few. He is a professional man, yet is constantly seeking new experiences and being frustrated. I found this an interesting point, as other people subsequently mentioned to me that adults in their family displayed symptoms similar to those of their hyperactive child.

Philip

Philip's family is large by today's standards. There are six children, now all adults. They were born at three-year intervals, with Philip the fifth child and the youngest boy of the family. His father is a doctor and his mother a nurse. Philip's arrival made the household rather crowded but the older children were out of the house at school or at nursery class during the day time. After his birth his mother felt very tired and later needed an operation. Philip was no small addition to the family as he weighed 12 pounds at birth.

His mother remembers him as active and lively from the start and she has some theories as to why he behaved as he did. She wonders if the small walled garden, with high gates through which the older children disappeared each day to the wider world beyond, proved restricting to him. She also felt that she had exhausted all her maternal energies on the earlier children and had lost her appetite for inventing new games and activities. Philip was the first child in their family to have a television to watch, as they acquired a set for the wedding of the Queen and Prince Philip. From his earliest days he sat in his high chair looking at the television. His mother wonders if the stimulation from this may have contributed to his abundant energy once he became more mobile.

'Today he would no doubt be labelled "hyperactive". He needed little sleep and was always the first person in the house to wake up, often as early as five in the morning, when he would immediately get up and rouse his brothers.'

At three years old he could read, so once he began school with 50 other five year-olds, whenever his restlessness disrupted the class the newly qualified teacher would banish him to a corner of the classroom and tell him to read.

'He returned home each day like a lion refreshed and roared about the house, jumping and climbing trees and tormenting his brothers and sister,' his mother remembers with a shudder.

As he grew older he found new ways of using up his excess energy. His chosen school friends lived on farms and he would spend every weekend with them, working from dawn to dusk, cleaning stables, carting bales and so on. At 15 he discovered sailing and thereafter devoted all his time to that activity, becoming a sea cadet at 16. Outside his home and school he never seemed to be regarded as inappropriately active, but at home there were times when he nearly drove the rest of the family mad. His mother feels that he needed the extra space to give him the opportunity to satisfy his urge to be active all the time. Even now, at 30 years of age, he is always on the go, despite a demanding job at sea. Whenever he is at home he will embark on some job of major house conversion or garden planning.

'In my view, "hyperactivity" is a subjective term applied to a child who reacts against his environment through sheer frustration,' suggests his mother. 'The cause of the extra need for physical activity may be overstimulation which in turn may have a physical cause such as diet, enzymes, or brain malfunction. It may be discovered and remedied, or it may be an inherited personality trait which is developed and aggravated by environmental factors – possibly overstimulation by the parents or siblings at some time of the day, followed by withdrawal when they are tired by the demands made on them to amuse and entertain the child.

'I am very puzzled by some of the children described as hyperactive today,' she adds. 'In some cases, not enough attention seems to be paid to all the possible causes, particularly if they are of average or above average intelligence.'

8 Hyperactivity Combined with Mental Handicap

Hyperactivity seems to be more prevalent amongst children and adults who are mentally handicapped. It is usually assumed to be a result of brain damage associated with their handicap; I wonder, however, if at least some could be helped by finding the cause of their hyperactivity, rather than concluding that it is inseparable from their handicap. I should like briefly to consider three mentally handicapped people, two of whom did not receive relief for their hyperactivity and one whose mother has been able to effect an improvement in his condition through thought and planning.

Cecilia
When I first met Cecilia she could walk and was about 18 months old. At the time her parents had not been told that she had Down's Syndrome and it came as a huge shock a little later to hear that she would not grow up normally.

Cecilia never stopped racing around. Her parents quickly abandoned the idea of having a beautiful home with ornaments or vases of flowers. She moved everything and broke anything within reach. Even the table cloth landed on the floor as soon as she had eaten her meal, taking the rest of the plates with it. She slept very little, her mother remembers. She wanted to bath and dress all her dolls each night before bed, and then in the middle of the night she would join her parents, wanting them to play with the dolls again. She would awake at the crack of dawn and remain active throughout the day, running in and out of the house and round the garden. Although she had a very loving nature, she would suddenly snatch at someone's spectacles or grab him by the hair and tug with all her might. She could not control her bladder or bowels. The family soon moved further into the country, to a house surrounded by fields, so that when she escaped from the garden she would not meet the danger of traffic. Eventually she became too much for her parents to cope with and, although they adored her, they had to place her in a hospital. When she was little there were only the two alternatives, with no support available for the parents if they kept the child at home.

At the time my family knew little about Down's Syndrome and thought that her overactive behaviour was part of her condition. Since then we have met numerous Down's children who are not overactive. Had Cecilia's parents found a way of dealing with her sleeplessness and speed they would undoubtedly have been able to keep her at home, so avoiding the heartbreak of parting.

Years later I renewed my acquaintance with Cecilia who is now an adult. She has slowed down and is kind and loving, a generous person and a pleasure to be with. Her speech, very limited as a child, is still developing and she loves to have visitors to talk to and someone to admire all her possessions. Ironically, her main problem is now one of immobility, as she has leg and hip problems developing which make it difficult for her to walk.

Christopher

This young man is 18 years old. He is severely mentally handicapped from an unknown cause. There are two younger children in the family. His mother remembers that from birth Chris had difficulty feeding and was very restless, waking often in the night. He began head banging from an early age, hitting his ears and forehead and eventually breaking his nose more than once. He sat up and learned to walk at about the normal time for a child, but having learned to walk, his mother began to wish that he had not become mobile! He spent all his time running and climbing; if a door or window stood open he would run away aimlessly and often escaped naked apart from a part of wellingtons.

Trying to make life as normal as possible for the family proved difficult. His mother remembers tethering him to the car bumper by a long rope to prevent him running away while they had a picnic. At night she had to lock him in his bedroom to prevent him reaching the kitchen while they slept. He enjoyed emptying all the cupboards onto the floor and taking everything out of the fridge, including milk bottles, which he broke. In the lounge all the furniture had to be placed so that he could not walk from one piece of furniture onto another and he needed constant attention to see that he came to no harm.

At seven years old Chris began school at an ESN (S) school in the grounds of a hospital for mentally handicapped people. He also began to spend the weekends on one of the wards.

'What a relief this was – for the first time in seven years to have a complete night's rest,' says his mother.

Gradually he began to stay at the hospital more often and eventually he moved in full time. Now the order is reversed: he spends time at home at the weekends and his brother and sister welcome his visits as the family are more able to cope with him when he is not permanently at home. They are all exhausted by the time he returns to the hospital, for he is very demanding and will drag them on five-mile walks to use up his energy, but everyone finds the present arrangements suit them best.

Kendal

Kendal went to live with his foster mother at eight weeks. He bore marks from a forceps delivery. Apparently both his parents were of low mental ability and his father also had a physical handicap. Little Kendal developed paralysis down his left side and his eyes bulged from the age of six months. The original plan had been for him to be adopted, but as the extent of his handicap showed up everyone realised that this would be abandoned and he would remain in care as a foster child.

At first Kendal could not keep his feeds down. Nothing helped this until his foster mother put him onto goat's milk. Then he began to thrive and gain weight, although he still vomited fairly frequently. He did not sleep for more than four hours out of 24. When he reached two years of age, his foster mother made a discovery: if he did not eat anything with artificial red or yellow colouring in it he ceased to vomit. Spurred on by this success, she removed all colourings and preservatives from his diet and not only did he become much calmer but his limbs relaxed so that they could be moved. At the time of his second birthday he could neither sit up nor turn over, but after three months on his new diet the physio-therapist could work on him much better and within six months he could sit and stand. Work continued on him for six hours each day and by the age of three he could walk. He is now six years old and can run and climb stairs. He is able to feed himself quite well and also plays. He cannot speak but is learning Makaton sign vocabulary at his school. His mother has just begun to teach him to swim, and within nine weeks of starting he had learnt to float and now kicks his arms and legs when told to do so.

Kendal has blond hair and blue eyes and his skin burns easily in the sun. He still does not sleep a full night, but sleeps for about six hours and wakes about three times in the night. His mother says that he tends to be restless and he drinks often. This is the diet his mother feeds him at present: fresh vegetables only, not tinned or frozen; no tomatoes or peas; no sugar or sweets or tinned fruit; fresh meat, not frozen, and sausages and beefburgers made specially for him without colouring or preservatives; goat's cheese; no jam or other spreads.

It would seem well worth the effort if parents with mentally handicapped children who are hyperactive or share some of the symptoms of this problem would take time to consider factors which may be affecting the child's behaviour. Any improvements which can be made are surely worthwhile.

9 Children with Allergies and Hyperactivity

A number of parents told me about the allergy problems from which their hyperactive children suffered. From a young age some had asthma, eczema, sore eyes, severe rashes, or continuous ear, nose and throat problems. Later it transpired that their hyperactivity was triggered by sensitivity either to colourings and preservatives in processed foods or to such foods as eggs, milk, pork, or beef.

Keith

Mrs Stone recalls that her son Keith had problems from birth. During the birth, forceps and vacuum extraction were used. Keith cried so much in the hospital that the nurses were unable to put him in with the other babies. When he came home he slept for only two to four hours during a 24-hour period. Until he reached five months no one in the family had one decent night's sleep.

Keith walked at ten months and spoke quite early. As he grew a little older he developed asthma – he wheezed, had headaches, vomited frequently and always looked pale. He had a constant thirst and did not gain weight as he should. By the time he was ten his mother no longer dared take him to the doctor any more as she could see by the doctor's reaction that he thought, 'Not her again.' She had the strong impression that he viewed her as a neurotic mother, yet she knew that there were genuine reasons for her concern.

The extent of Keith's hyperactive problem can be seen from the following story. One evening the Stones were invited to a friend's home and Keith was put in his pram to sleep in the hall. Instead of sleeping he screamed so loudly that they had to pick him up so that he would not waken their host's children. To keep him occupied they put him in a baby bouncer, but whenever they tried to get him to sleep he started screaming again. He bounced and bounced all evening. Their friends said that it made them tired to watch him, but he kept bouncing until the early hours of the morning.

By the time he reached the age of two Mrs Stone felt like a zombie through lack of sleep. Her mother came to her aid and suggested that she stay in bed for a week and get as much rest as possible. Keith went home with his grandmother, but three days later Mrs Stone's mother returned with him saying, 'Please have him back. I can't stand it any longer. If you don't have him back I'm afraid that my marriage will break up.'

Keith had cried continuously as usual, had refused to allow his grandfather to sleep with his grandmother and had generally worn them out completely.

As Keith grew older and mixed with other children, his mother noticed that he tended to be quiet in a group. He also lacked confidence to carry out instructions. When Keith was ten a new headmaster took over the school which he attended. He liked Keith, thought him bright and promising and made a fuss of him. He used rewards to encourage him to carry out tasks. On one occasion, however, he failed to keep a promise to Keith to allow him to deliver Harvest Festival produce to the old people near the school. Keith became very upset and ran away from the school. The headmaster felt that Keith's problems lay at home. Mrs Stone thinks that the headmaster went to see her doctor about the boy and the whole issue became confused. The doctor did not prove at all helpful at the time, yet later, when Mrs Stone visited the surgery, he asked her to bring a urine sample quickly and to post a form to the hospital on the way home. The sudden urgency following his indifference alarmed her.

At the hospital appointment the doctor asked Keith to remove his trousers. As he did not respond to this request the doctor said he would contact the psychiatrist. In front of Keith he stated that he thought the boy had a mental problem and wanted him admitted to hospital. His parents would not agree to this.

Then Mrs Stone heard a talk on the radio about hyperactivity.

It made her think. The description of the mood changes, with the child sometimes happy and at other times rude and unco-operative, could have been a description of Keith. She wrote in to the programme and as a result joined the Hyperactive Children's Support Group. For three months the whole family followed the suggested food programme and Keith settled down well. When she tried to re-introduce certain foods into his diet, it upset him. Keith's worst reaction was to orange squash. After drinking it on one occasion he attacked someone with a knife, which his mother feels is a strong indication that colourings added to products are a main cause of his problem. At first he cheated on the diet, but his behaviour then returned to the pre-diet state and he soon realised that the cheating was not worthwhile.

'We decided to punish him if he misbehaved,' Mrs Stone told me, 'and not allow him to get away with bad behaviour because he had eaten something forbidden. Now he sees that it is not worth cheating if he is punished as a result.'

Keith cannot tolerate aspirin and vomits if he takes it. He also vomits after eating natural foods which do not agree with him, and it has been a matter of trial and error for his family to find out which they are. His mood changes noticeably after he has eaten chocolate. The family live in a beautiful home, but some of the doors have holes in them and the bathroom has broken tiles which are reminders of Keith's destructive behaviour in the past. He used to lock himself in the bathroom, so the keys had to be removed, making it impossible for him to stay in there and attack the room.

The Stones' doctor refused to give Keith medicine without colouring, but a herbalist provided an alternative. Keith now enjoys a varied diet. His mother makes her own bread as she finds that his behaviour alters after eating bread from the local baker, even though it is supposed to have no additives. The local butcher makes up special sausages without preservatives and has five or six customers who buy them for children with a similar problem.

'I do not find the diet easy,' says Mrs Stone. 'It is time-consuming and expensive and the shops are not geared up to our requirements.' But she adds, 'If you are concerned enough about a child, you will try it.'

As well as the food programme she is trying the use of Evening Primrose Oil with Keith and sees good results from its use. She advises other parents to try one thing at a time in order to avoid confusion by attempting to do everything at once.

'This problem can split families,' says Mrs Stone. 'There is also a danger of being over protective and stifling such children. Some members of the family may insist that the child just needs a good hiding to sort him out. Different points of view can cause great disharmony while families seek to find an answer to the child's problems.'

John

All the members of the Stewart family suffer from allergies of the kind which are readily recognised. Their son John has had the most problems, yet at first they were not thought to be linked with allergies. John's birth had no complications, but for the first six months of his life he suffered with colic. As a small child he had constant colds, throat infections and ear problems. At four and five years of age he had operations to remove cysts from his ears. Until he was five years old he wet the bed. He constantly complained of aching arms and legs, stomach pains and tiredness. He had red, sore eyes for which he received treatment from the family doctor and also hospital treatment. (Later his mother found that tobacco smoke caused this problem). Until the age of nine he had to take antibiotics every three weeks or so. He had his tonsils removed when he was nine years old and then developed chronic catarrh which lasted all year round. The doctor continued to give him antibiotics and when Mrs Stewart tried to discuss his poor health he told her that John would grow out of the problem. She felt that the doctor regarded her as an overanxious mother. Her family, too, felt that she showed overanxiety about his health and that she lacked firmness with John. His sisters, two years older, had some problems too, with aching limbs and stomach pains, feelings of tiredness and of having a permanent cold.

John experienced learning difficulties at school. He could not sit still and concentrate, was constantly 'twitching' and talked to himself non-stop in a loud voice, making no attempt to communicate with anyone. At night he snored loudly and cried out in his sleep. Despite the fact that he ate little, he grew fat and became a miserable and difficult child.

When John reached 12 years of age the family decided to try changing his diet to see if this might help him, as nothing else seemed to have had any effect. Within two months they noticed a difference in his behaviour. He stopped talking non-stop and was less difficult and twitchy. Encouraged by this improvement, and having read the book *Not all in the Mind* (Mackarness), Mrs Stewart decided to track down any possible food sensitivities he might have. A local doctor had an allergy clinic so she sought his help. She came away with a prescription for a coloured cough mixture and a spray for John's catarrh (although for some time his diet had excluded food containing artificial colour). The medicine could not be used and the spray did not seem to help. Eventually, by trial and error, Mrs Stewart found that citrus fruit caused the catarrh and that beans and oats made him twitchy.

Last year the family decided to have desensitising treatment for their food problems. This is not yet available on the National Health Service and is very expensive. Their diet had become too limited and this treatment seemed to offer the chance of a more normal diet. John has been desensitised for 16 foods and his sister for 14. They also had hair analysis which revealed that the whole family lacked essential minerals. They have to pay for the supplements they take as their doctor is not willing to prescribe them.

'I think it is appalling that nobody suggested John's health problems might be caused by allergy,' says his mother. 'I was always careful to mention that we have allergies in the family such as hay fever, but over the years, having seen many doctors and hospitals for various conditions, not once was allergy mentioned or considered.'

The health of the whole family has now improved. Mrs Stewart is delighted that her own problems, which had persisted for more than 20 years – cystitis and a feeling of 'illness all over' which had led to a complete breakdown in health several years before – have also been rectified as a result of treating the cause rather than the symptoms. All the family now enjoy excellent health and rarely have even a cold.

'Our remaining concern is that our son has not been able to catch up with the education that he lost as a result of his problems,' comments his mother. 'At the age of 15 he has a reading age of 12, but considering that at nine he could hardly read at all, that is not too bad. His spelling is terrible, he has a bad memory and has never been able to remember maths tables. However there are encouraging signs, for he is doing well in metal work, art and physics.

Rosemary

This little girl is fortunate to be alive, indeed the chances of her being born at all were, to say the least, somewhat slim. Her mother already had one child, but she miscarries very easily and Rosemary was the result of her fourth pregnancy. When pregnant with Rosemary she threatened to miscarry at six weeks and needed three weeks in hospital with complete bed rest. When 12 weeks pregnant she again went into hospital and continued to be in and out of hospital until the 22nd week of pregnancy, when it was felt that she had a good chance of keeping the baby. She also received tests to make sure that the baby was not malformed and naturally trying to abort. At about 23 weeks her blood pressure rocketed and remained high until Rosemary arrived. Throughout the whole pregnancy she suffered from nausea due to an imbalance in hormones which had been the root cause of her previous miscarriages. She had drug treatment for this throughout the pregnancy. Finally Rosemary arrived six weeks prematurely after a 40-hour labour. She weighed 5 lb 4 oz but needed care in an incubator for a while, and for the first six hours of her life it seemed unlikely that she would survive. After a further week in intensive care she went home.

Rosemary's mother noticed that she had a very sensitive skin with patches of eczema, although this caused little trouble until she reached three years of age. Various creams were tried but eventually her chest and tummy became raw and weeping and the doctor decided to send her to a skin specialist. There had, however, been other problems with Rosemary almost from the beginning.

'The first week I had her home she slept all the time, but then it started – crying, never sleeping in the daytime and only

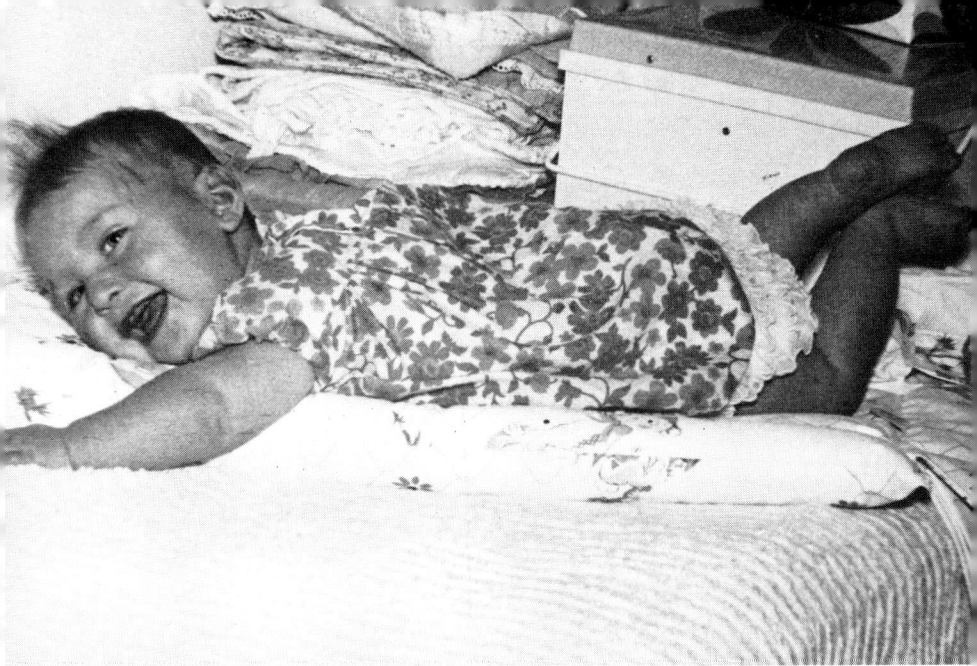

Tanya, an apparently normal and happy baby.

Ready to explore.

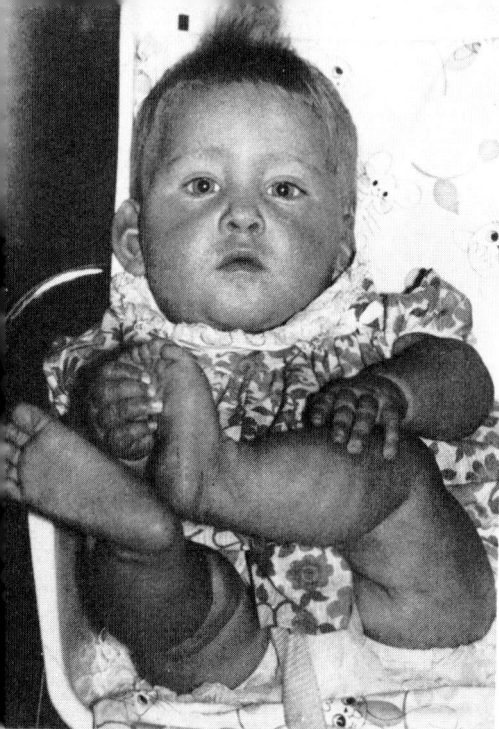

In a pensive mood.

The apple of her daddy's eye.

On the village green . . .

. . . where we spent much of our time.

Not too sure of this . . .

. . . or this.

Above: A little reassurance from mum.

Left: Hurry up, before I fall off the fence!

Above right: A new game?

Above far right: Posing for the camera before dashing off with teddy.

Right: Move over, John!

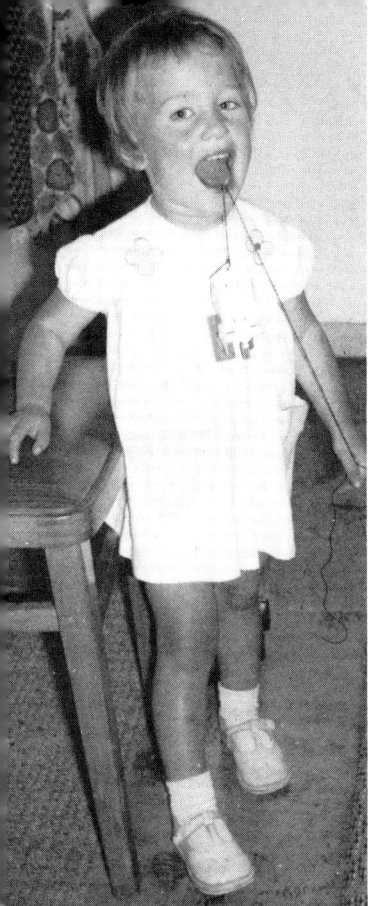

Left: Ready, steady . . .

Below: GO!

Just before *he* took *her* for a walk.

A favourite occupation.

A rainy day beside the Thames.

Familiar chaos in Tanya's bedroom.

Why does it get in such a mess??

Ah, that's better. I'll try to keep it tidy now.

Ever on the go . . .

Up –

Down –

Jumping –

Upside down.

A song with mother. (*By permission of The Maidenhead Advertiser*.)

Inspired by Jim, Tanya walked 9 miles. (*By permission of the Bracknell News*)

OTHER PARENTS' PROBLEMS

Going for a ride, Simon?   Whoops!

An upside down view of life.

And that can go!

Right: Gina and her dog at the dog show.

Below left: Sufficient concentration to build a tower . . .

Below right: But that is the end of the game.

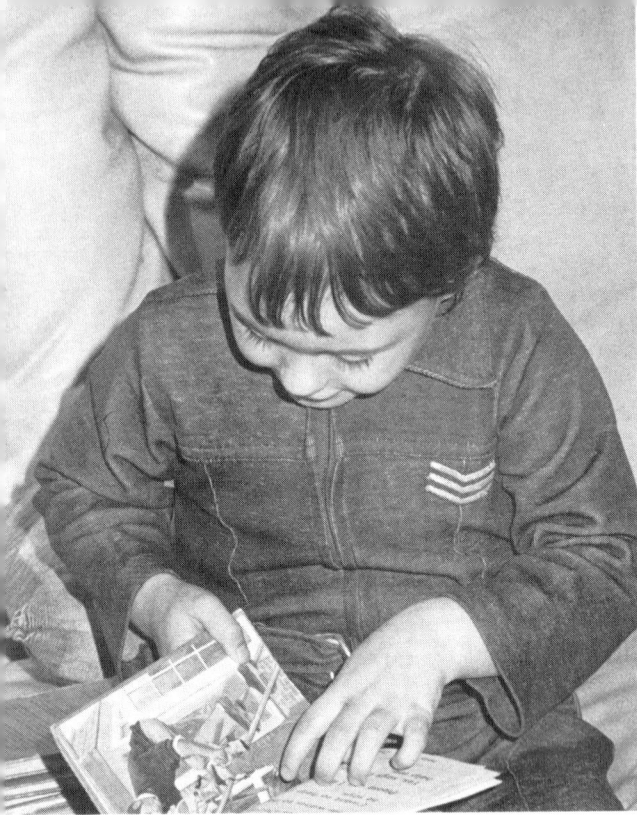

A brief look at a book . . .

And Nigel is off again.

Tense and keyed up.

Encouragement from big sister.

A quick kiss for mum.

sleeping for one hour at a time at night,' remembers her mother. She continued to be an angry baby and grew into a frustrated toddler. She seemed to want to do things beyond her capability and had tantrums when she could not achieve what she wanted. Because of her swings of temperament her parents felt apprehensive about going anywhere with her. As a toddler she screamed if put in her pushchair, but if she was allowed to walk she would run about and then fall over, after which everyone suffered, as she cried and whined for the rest of the day. Although she slept more as she grew older, she still woke 10 or 12 times a night. Despite her strange temperament her mother noticed that she needed a great deal of loving.

The family sought help from the doctor, but nothing constructive was forthcoming. Her mother remembers the advice she received at various times, both from doctors and others:

'All children are lively.'

'You must expect this if you have children.'

'We have the same problem – you are not the only one.'

'You seem to feel sorry for yourself.'

'You cannot expect all children to be alike.'

'It is the way you are approaching parenthood.'

'You probably have the baby blues.' (Rosemary was then two-and-a-half.)

'Have some Valium – if you calm down the child will too.'

Relatives accepted that Rosemary seemed difficult and needed careful handling, but they found it hard to believe that the family could have one normal, polite, very intelligent, placid and patient child and then produce such a horror the second time round. Real friends, too, accepted that the child had difficulties and did not blame the parents. They tried to help by taking Rosemary out for walks to give her mother a rest.

Until Rosemary reached three-and-a-half years of age nothing seemed to help her. Even with sleeping drugs her sleep did not improve. Her mother had to put up with the problems and exercised all the patience she possessed, but she lost over a stone in weight through worry and lack of sleep.

Then the family took Rosemary to the skin specialist as

suggested by the doctor. He thought that her diet could be causing the severe outbreak of eczema and gave them a diet which excluded colouring and preservatives in food.

'Within one week her skin improved tremendously,' says her mother, 'and after two weeks the eczema had disappeared. I also noticed that she had improved in herself and slept for longer periods at night. After three weeks she was sleeping all night, every night, and was a happy and contented child, suddenly achieving things she had been unable to do before. She could learn a lot quicker, had a lot more patience and – lo and behold – no more frustration or tantrums!

'After two months I decided to see if the improvement was just coincidence, so I introduced to her diet a few things that had been cut out and again she became a horrible child and covered in eczema.'

Educationally Rosemary is now a very bright four-and-a-half year-old, and has started to read, write and do simple arithmetic. At present she attends nursery school in the mornings and loves being there; she is keen to start school as she has a constant desire to learn. Her mother praises the staff for faithfully maintaining her diet and not giving her anything to eat but the special biscuits that they keep for her:

'It makes life so much easier for parents if there is co-operation from others who care for a child for part of the day.'

Doctors who see Rosemary are still largely sceptical, however.

'They agree wholeheartedly that the diet has cured her eczema', says her mother, 'it is a visible thing, after all. But they are still reluctant to accept that it is the diet which calmed down her hyperactivity. One or two of the younger doctors are showing signs of believing this, however.'

Exactly what Rosemary reacts to is not certain. Her mother has not tested her to see whether it is preservatives in food or a particular colour that is added to food. She just gives her as natural a diet as possible and cuts out most preservatives and colourings, and is thankful that this seems to provide an answer to Rosemary's problems.

Dorian and Paul

Maureen's two sons have both presented problems. Dorian, who is now seven, had a forceps delivery 24 hours after Maureen's waters broke. He needed care in a special unit for two weeks after his birth as he failed to thrive. His mother wonders if this happened because of the amount of Pethidine she received during labour. She took him home on the 16th day and bottle fed him, as she had not been allowed to give him breast milk while in the special unit since it had been blood stained when expressed. At home he began to gain weight and by eight months weighed over 23 pounds. He talked at 16 months but did not walk until 19 months.

During the night Dorian slept well but woke between three and five times, going back to sleep after he had had a drink. During the day he would remain sitting most of the time, being almost depressed and very tearful, or else having tantrums. He was not in fact hyperactive in one sense, but his temperament showed great similarity to a hyperactive child. His mother now realises that he is hypoactive rather than hyperactive, but she feels that it is as difficult to live with from day to day. When Dorian's problems showed up Maureen had no one to help her cope with him, but was told that he seemed to be a late developer.

Dorian developed asthma quite young. He wheezed at night and had a blocked nose in the daytime. He received treatment for these symptoms and for the colds which he kept catching, but no one suggested that there might be an underlying cause to his health problems which persisted until he started going to play school. He did not enjoy going there at all and the teacher said that he seemed withdrawn. At five years old, when he began school, his teacher described him as very difficult and lacking concentration to learn.

About a year ago Maureen heard about an allergy testing service. She took Dorian for tests and the results showed that he had an allergy to milk and all milk products and also beef. She left these things out of his diet and he showed a very marked improvement.

'I found his behaviour much better and his school work also improved,' she says. 'He has caught up in school and in reading and has even overtaken many of the other children.'

Tests also show that he has environmental allergies to mattress mite and house dust, so he still suffers from nasal congestion. In addition he is enuretic by day and night, which has caused him many problems at school. However Maureen is receiving advice from the allergy clinic. It is thought that beet and cane sugar cause this trouble so he now has medicinal glucose or fructose instead of sugar. Maureen notices that after three days without sugar he begins to be dry at night and then he becomes dry in the daytime. If a mistake is made in his diet and he has sugar accidentally, then he begins wetting again.

Maureen's second son, Paul, is now four, three years younger than his brother. He also had problems at his birth. During labour the umbilical cord was found to be knotted around his neck. Each time Maureen had a contraction and pushed, the cord tightened around his neck. Paul spent 24 hours in a special unit as a result of this problem. Maureen did manage to fulfil her wish to breastfeed with Paul and continued to do so for four-and-a-half months. When she began to give him mixed feeds during the day he became restless and cried often. During the night he would wake up six or seven times wanting something to drink. The older he grew the more restless he became. He had poor concentration and co-ordination and became very destructive.

Maureen took Paul to the same clinic as his brother. Tests on him showed that wheat in his diet caused problems, and since being on a wheat-free diet he has definitely improved. He is able to sleep right through the night and he is not thirsty as before. His co-ordination is better and he is less destructive. His concentration has improved so much that he is able to do 50-piece jig-saw puzzles without help.

'If he eats anything which has wheat in it he screams for ages and reverts to his old behaviour day and night, and he becomes very thirsty,' observes his mother.

Having found answers to her children's problems Maureen now helps to run a self-help group for mothers with hyperactive children and children with allergies.

Gina
This little girl is blonde and blue eyed and seems exceptionally

bright, although her mother notices that she does odd things such as putting clothes on back to front, starting a book at the back and saying that backwards is forwards. She is nearly four years old but has had many problems during her short life.

For the first week of her life everything went well and her family really enjoyed having her. Then the difficulties began. She began to take up to two hours to finish her feed (bottle) and afterwards would not lie on her tummy or back. If left lying she screamed for up to three hours. Her mother, Janet, found that the only way to keep her quiet was to carry her around strapped in an upright position to her front and even then she rarely seemed completely happy. When she did go to sleep for a short while the slightest sound or movement would wake her again. For the first three months everyone thought that Gina had permanent colic, but during the next three months she seemed to get worse and Janet became more and more depressed and tired. At six months Gina slept for four nights and the family thought that the breakthrough had come. Unfortunately the rejoicing proved to be premature; after this Gina's behaviour became impossible: she went back to waking every two or three hours at least, could not keep still for any length of time or play with anything without becoming frustrated with it, and she refused to be left alone.

At about six months, too, Gina developed an allergic condition. Her eyes became very sore, particularly at night. The doctor and the health visitor said that it was caused by sunlight. They told Janet to stop worrying about Gina and being neurotic. She should take Valium and in a couple of weeks she would be feeling fine and all would be well!

Some time later Janet met a friend who told her that a relative's child had had a similar eye condition and suggested that perhaps Gina had a milk allergy.

'I cut out milk and dairy products and the results were incredible,' says her mother. 'As long as she sticks to this diet then her eyes are fine.'

They noticed that oranges had a similar effect on Gina, but they did not realise until later that she also showed sensitivity to colourings, flavourings and preservatives in foods.

After Gina's eye problems stopped it took her about 18

months to realise that closing her eyes to go to sleep would not make them hurt. In the meantime, her hyperactivity grew steadily worse. As she grew older she showed her frustrations more and more and became angry when she did not fall asleep. Even when she did sleep she would wake up six to ten times a night.

'Often, after about 11 o'clock at night, she would be screaming and sobbing uncontrollably and at times would refuse to be touched,' Janet remembers. 'She just writhed around on the bed or the floor. Gina never woke without crying and because of a lack of sleep she was always grumpy, cried a lot in the day, couldn't concentrate and, apart from the fact that she demanded and gave a lot of love, was not we felt, a very nice child to have arround.'

Gina was over three years old when Janet found that artificial additives in her diet were largely the cause of her problems. So long as her diet is now kept free of these Gina and her family can at last enjoy a normal life.

Daniel

The *Nursing Times* published an article about Daniel written by his mother, Diana Wells, entitled 'Daniel's Allergies' (*Nursing Times*, May 19th, 1982). Since then she has also written a recipe book to help parents of other children who need special diets. It is called *What shall I give him today?* and contains 50 milk, egg and additive-free recipes (see book list). Prior to the birth of her children Mrs Wells practised as a health visitor.

In correspondence with me, Mrs Wells said:

'Daniel's hyperactive problems have undoubtedly been grossly aggravated by his allergies, and as we learn more about them and can eliminate the offending foods, so his hyperactivity is being controlled.'

Mrs Wells is a contact in her area for the Hyperactive Children's Support Group.

'I felt the need to help others who are in the same difficult situation that we have lived through,' she says. 'I feel that the support of "self help groups" is invaluable.'

Daniel had a normal birth following a trouble-free pregnancy. His mother breastfed him for the first five months and noticed that a rash appeared during his feeds but faded before the next feed. Having read about cow's milk allergy in breastfed babies, she tried leaving milk products out of her own diet and within a few weeks he ceased to have the rash. It was later, when she began to give him mixed feeds, that very severe problems appeared. Certain food brought up a rash at once and half a teaspoonful of a certain baby food produced a violent reaction:

'He vomited copiously and urticaria appeared immediately, initially around mouth and neck, then spreading to trunk and limbs. His face swelled and a stridor developed. He had difficulty in breathing, and his colour rapidly deteriorated.' Her doctor advised her on the telephone to take him to the hospital.

'By the time I arrived, his condition had improved and, although the urticaria was evident and there was still some stridor, there was obviously no danger.' (*Nursing Times*.)

Later a paediatrician confirmed cow's milk allergy after taking a detailed history of the baby. He told Mrs Wells that children usually grow out of such conditions by the age of 18 months. I have since spoken to a doctor specialising in allergies who feels that this view is not valid. He suggests that although it may appear to have gone, it may in fact be a masking effect which can cause other problems as the years go by.

As Daniel grew older his poor sleeping caused the family problems. During the night he would wake eight or nine times asking for drinks. This became exhausting for them, but they could find nothing that would help him sleep through the night without disturbing them. Then Mrs Wells began to wonder about his diet and tried giving him fresh fruit juice instead of a proprietary blackcurrant juice which contained artificial colouring and flavouring. Very soon he was sleeping throughout the night and she also noticed that his behaviour had altered. At this time Daniel was not yet two years old.

'He was less excitable, much more amenable, and had more control over his temper. In fact he was a different child. We wrote to the Hyperactive Children's Support Group to ask for any help and advice they could give us, and obtained the Feingold Diet sheet which we have adhered to ever since. This diet consists simply of foods free from artificial additives, and is based mainly on fresh foods.' (*Nursing Times.*)

Later they discovered exactly which food items have an adverse effect on Daniel. Fruit containing natural salicylate causes his behaviour problems and artificial colour has other severe effects. He even reacted to the dye which came out of a new sponge used in his bath. His face became swollen and he woke up very frightened the same night. For a while he could not breathe through his nose. On one occasion he accidentally spilt a little milk left by a visitor; at once a rash developed on the parts of his body touched by the milk.

Daniel went to a children's hospital and received tests for his allergies.

'The tests also showed that his immune system has failed to mature yet, and that he is producing substances in his blood which are responsible for all these allergies. As so little is known about the immune system, we have been told that it is difficult to predict the future with any certainty, and that indeed the doctors are learning all the time from situations such as Daniel's.' (*Nursing Times.*)

Daniel's appetite is very variable. Sometimes he will eat very little and he is very suspicious of any food that he has not tried before. It is suggested that this is because he has found that he has bad reactions to food and is consequently suspicious of eating. As he even gets reactions from accidental splashes from any dairy products his suspicions are quite justified. His parents have to be extremely careful when they are not with him, as other people do not realise how serious a problem this can be. His mother has made him badges to wear at play group stating, 'I am violently allergic to many foods,' or 'Serious food allergies. Please do not feed me,' in order to remind people of his problem or to stop anyone who may not know from giving him something which will cause him difficulties. He also wears a Medic-alert bracelet in case of emergency.

Daniel has a younger brother who also has some food-related problems. The doctor advises caution in the feeding of the younger child because of his brother's difficulties. He is also having tests done as a precaution. Before he reached 18 months some foods would pass through his body undigested or cause him to have very loose stools.

'As a practising health visitor before I had the children,' says Mrs Wells, 'I was, of course, aware of the problems I have mentioned throughout this article (*Nursing Times*), but what a wealth of experience I have accrued over the past three years, and how much more shall I be able to offer my families when I return to health visiting.'

Rupert

Recently I met a young man of 19 and his family. They wish that his problem had been diagnosed early in his life, for, since a full diagnosis and correct help were not available then, he has suffered very many serious problems which have caused trouble to his family, his friends, the schools he attended, and could have ruined his life totally. Fortunately, not all is lost and now life is beginning to offer him opportunities which he earlier missed because of the difficulties he encountered. His problems were extreme and hopefully not too many other people will encounter the same difficulties, but his family would like other people to know of their story so that some may be saved the suffering they have experienced. His case is being very carefully examined by doctors and articles have been published about him.

Rupert always had a runny nose and eczema. Between four and five years of age he was found to have allergies to dust mite and cats. Later he received desensitising treatment for these allergies. However, since birth he had experienced other problems as well: he fed poorly and cried a great deal. By the time he was one year old a doctor had labelled him as hyperactive. His family did not fully know the meaning of this. He slept little and was busy all the time when awake. He needed adult supervision constantly as he would write on the walls and had many accidents.

From a young age it seemed that Rupert had enormous potential educationally. He gathered large amounts of general knowledge, yet at school he tended to play around all the time and not concentrate on learning. For example, he would stand on his head to see how long he could remain there before the teacher told him to stop. Some people said that he was too bright and so became easily bored by school work which he found far too easy for him. At home he happily listened to his mother reading long and involved stories, but at school he never fulfilled expectations because he did not work.

On one occasion, when he was ten, he went shoplifting and was caught. His mother thinks that being caught prevented further repetitions. His parents had to live abroad and he went to a public school where at 13 years of age, without their knowledge, he began smoking and drinking. He was also introduced to the drug scene. It became necessary to move him to another school because problems arose over discipline.

While he was attending the new school, a staff member wrote to Rupert's parents telling them about his extreme changes of mood. It was felt that they should know about this and obtain some treatment for him. Then, at the age of 16, while on holiday with his parents in Pakistan, he became very ill with a stomach 'bug'. On his return to school the problem persisted, so he went onto a diet for a week. He received only water and fruit during this time. Suddenly his character changed completely. He wrote the most wonderful letter to his parents expressing things that he had never mentioned before. The change appeared so dramatic that it could only have been as a result of the diet. His mother flew back from Pakistan and studied all that she could find on food allergies. She made contact with a doctor who specialised in allergies and, although he had just retired, he agreed to help Rupert. He did tests on him and found that he still had the allergy to cats and dust and also to eggs and milk. During his next holiday in Pakistan Rupert went on a diet which excluded eggs and milk and, incidentally, pork as well, since it could not be obtained in Pakistan. He improved a great deal on this diet.

After the holiday Rupert returned to school only to become terribly ill. The school had agreed to follow the diet but it proved difficult where so much food had to be prepared. He lost a stone in weight, wandered at night and smashed windows. The matter became so serious that his mother had to fly to England again to sort things out. Arrangements were made for his food to be cooked in separate saucepans.

At this time he began to experiment with alcohol again and had by now developed an intolerance to it. He also began to take drugs. Everyone expected him to win a scholarship to

Cambridge but he failed and had a mental breakdown. Once more his mother returned from Pakistan to visit him in hospital. Whilst there he did not receive the correct diet and deteriorated rapidly, becoming completely mad; he broke into a drug cupboard, took a mixture of drugs and almost killed himself. His family asked permission to feed him themselves, but were told this could not be allowed, so they took the law into their own hands and stayed with him all day, feeding him the diet he should have so that he could not eat the hospital food. At the end of the week, when his behaviour had stabilised, they removed him from the hospital and arranged for him to become an out-patient at a London hospital where a psychologist helped him to plan a four-day rotation diet eliminating all his known allergens and caffeine. He was able to come off all medication. However, he again began drinking and taking drugs and ended up back in hospital where he was kept under sedation until his mother could return to England.

As Rupert appeared to have problems in assimilating his food, he began receiving digestive enzyme therapy. The enzymes had to be imported from America at a cost to his family of £1 per day. In Europe all enzymes originate from pigs and enzymes from ox are only available from the United States. It had become apparent that the lack of pork in his diet in Pakistan had been correct. He is now on a strict diet without eggs, milk or pork. In the daytime he receives no medication at all but has a little at night at present. He has held down two part-time jobs for the last six months and has been offered a full-time job later in the year.

As a result of Rupert's health problems his mother and sister have discovered that their health has also improved with the use of digestive enzymes and exclusion diets. His mother sees Rupert's problems as inherited, since she and his sister have lesser but similar difficulties with food intolerances. His uncle has also experienced problems with mental illness which began with difficulties in childhood and have worsened over the years.

'If only we had found treatment for him as a little child,' says Rupert's mother. 'As he suffered with diarrhoea as well as the other problems, diet and enzyme treatment at an early age could well have prevented all these difficulties we have gone through. It might be wise for parents in certain cases to check with their doctor regarding enzyme treatment. It could save them many problems later.'

10 Response by Hyperactive Children to a Change of Diet

Of the children discussed in this book, there are twelve who had no apparent allergy problems but were nevertheless hyperactive (one hypoactive); all of them have improved as a result of an alteration in their diet. The majority seem to have problems if they eat food containing additives. If they eat as natural a diet as possible, avoiding preservatives and colourings in processed foods, they experience an improvement in temperament and a slowing down of activity. A number of parents single out orange squash yet again as being a particular problem. Most soft drinks contain colouring – even the so-called blackcurrant health drinks – but possibly most children drink orange squash more than other drinks. It is also interesting to note that a number of these children had difficult births and that some mothers seem a little suspicious of Pethidine.

Tony

During labour Tony's mother, Mrs Williams, became dehydrated, and he eventually came into the world aided by the use of forceps. She remembers that he did not cry when born but made cooing sounds. As a young child he showed typically hyperactive behaviour and disliked contact. In fact, Mrs Williams remembers that even before his birth he seemed very active. By the time he was two-and-a-half years old his behaviour was causing his parents great concern and, in addition, as he grew older he did not become dry at night; although his parents tried everything – alarms, medicine from the doctor, getting him up several times in the night – nothing helped.

Just before Tony reached 11 years of age a doctor

recommended his mother to the Hyperactive Children's Support Group. Mrs Williams took their advice and put him on the suggested food programme. Within two weeks his family observed a definite improvement in his behaviour. For the sake of economy and ease the whole family adopted the food programme which avoids colourings, additives and preservatives in foods and certain natural foods containing salicylates. Mrs Williams notices that he is particularly sensitive to apples and chocolate but enjoys Carob Bars as an alternative to the chocolate.

After a number of very difficult years, it is a great relief to the family that they have been able to find a solution to Tony's problems. His mother told me some of the details:

'I breastfed Tony for three months. As he grew older he showed little interest in food and preferred breakfast cereal even to a hot dinner. He always seemed thirsty. From two-and-a-half he had sleeping problems, although as a baby he had been very sleepy. His brother, three years younger, is far more independent. Perhaps Tony would have been better with an older brother as he seems to need someone to look up to and does not readily accept the role of "big brother". He is not too kind to his little brother.'

I asked Mrs Williams how he progressed when he began school.

'Amazingly he has not been too great a problem at school, but his teacher says that he could achieve more. It seems to make him frustrated that he cannot reach his ideals, for he is a perfectionist in that respect. He does very detailed drawings but has poor reading ability. Tests show him to be about three years behind in reading and one year behind in comprehension.'

The worst problems manifested themselves at home:

'He has always had a good relationship with me, but within the family he relates badly. He has been known to pull all the buttons off his shirt, pull his mattress off the bed and throw it downstairs. If he had a clash of temperament with someone he would go into his room and tear up his own things. He even threatened me once by grabbing me by my collar and on another occasion punched me and his brother for no apparent reason. He began using bad language as a way of drawing attention to himself, and when we told him off he appeared not to hear or understand. When he was a little older, after a reprimand he would have tantrums, swear or be very badly behaved. We became very worried about this and did not want him to end up becoming a thug.'

As a result of these problems the family were directed to a psychologist. He suggested strict discipline, which they must enforce. They were to report back on the results. At the next visit, he suggested that they try giving him no discipline at all. His mother objected to this as she felt that Tony would become confused by these experiments. Moreover the psychologist was not keen for Tony to alter his eating habits to follow the Feingold food programme suggested by the Hyperactive Children's Support Group.

The family heard of a herbalist with experience in treating hyperactive children. He gave Tony herbal medicine and tablets which helped him over the problem of bed wetting, and since following his treatment Tony's diet has been widened. The herbalist thinks that he is not really hyperactive now but has behaviour problems left over from his earlier years.

Roger

Roger's mother commented to me that he is not the only hyperactive person in his family. His father finds it very difficult to 'unwind' and is always busy with something. This is also a characteristic of his father's other male relatives.

Roger is nearly eight years old now but has had problems since his birth. Again, as with Tony, his mother noticed that he seemed very active before birth. When she had a second son four years later she felt that something might be wrong with the baby as he did not move all the time! She had a long labour with Roger followed by a forceps delivery. From birth he slept poorly; when fed at midnight he took two hours to feed and settle to sleep, but would wake again at three. Having just settled by five, he would wake again for the next feed at six, and so on through the daytime. He kept up this wakefulness at night until recently, his mother says. His parents had to take turns to be with him at night, as once he learned to walk he would not stay in his bedroom and needed constant vigil. On one occasion, when they became too tired to cope, they allowed him to sleep with them, but they did not want to make this a permanent habit.

It helped the family when, at the age of three, Roger began to attend a private nursery. He progressed reasonably well depending on who cared for him. If a teacher expected the children to sit down and behave he found it impossible to obey. At home his parents coped with his temper tantrums by removing him from the situation – they would send him to his room where he would kick and scream for up to an hour. Then they heard that diet might help him and put him on the Feingold food programme for 18 months. During that time they discovered the individual foods which trigger his behaviour. Orange squash seemed to be the worst culprit. He now eats more or less the same as the rest of the family apart from a few items and does not have sweets.

As a result of these changes he can now sleep well and his mother is able to make up for all the sleep she lost over the years. Roger now goes to bed fairly early and sleeps until just before eight each morning. His mother admits that those years were very difficult but does not regret the experience.

'It has made me a different person,' she says. 'It gave me a lot of patience.'

She now helps other parents by organising regular meetings in her area with a crèche to enable mothers to attend during weekday morning meetings.

Nigel

Recently I met a young man with a double problem: hyperactivity and epilepsy. His mother told me how these had apparently arisen and about the difficulties they cause.

Nigel's birth was quite a normal one. He seemed to be an ordinary, active baby and had no sleeping problems, but when he was 18 months old he rammed a cotton wool bud into his ear. Immediately following this he changed from a normal placid child into a little horror. Within three months of the incident he became uncontrollable. He also appeared to be having epileptic fits and the family had to spend a lot of time going to and from the hospital.

His grandmother had had a great deal of experience with children and tended to think that his mother gave in to him too much. She offered to have him for a day to help out. At the end of the day she said, 'Never again.' She could not cope with him any better than his mother could.

The doctor recommended the Hyperactive Children's Support Group and its food programme. Within three or four weeks Nigel's parents noticed a great difference in his behaviour. Prior to the changes in his diet, whenever he was in hospital he had to be strapped into his cot, unless someone could sit with him all the time, to avoid injury by falling out. He has been on the programme for 18 months and having overcome the worst of one of his problems, the aim is now to control his fits. These are in fact so mild that their diagnosis is uncertain, although they seem likely to be epileptic.

'He seems to know when a fit is coming,' says his mother. 'He runs to me and hangs on tight, grinding his teeth. Then he goes blue for a short while and afterwards sleeps for a long time.'

One new problem is that the medication Nigel receives for the epilepsy quietens him for a while but then brings on a bout of overactivity, so that now a balance is being sought between controlling the epilepsy and reducing the hyperactivity. As a result of this he now has some problems with sleeping which he did not have earlier. Like many other hyperactive children, he is very thirsty and drinks a lot of milk.

Nigel is now nearly four years old. His speech is not good and he cannot hold a conversation. His mother compares it with the speech development of his older sisters and finds that it is similar to their speech at the age of two.

'I thought that he had good ability as he could count up to 100, but then I found that he cannot count objects. He goes to a diagnostic unit for children with various problems and will stay there until he is considered ready to go on to another school.'

Margaret

Margaret is one of three children. She is nearly 12 years old and has a brother of nine and a sister of six. No one ever suggested that she might be hyperactive but she has always been an extremely difficult child.

When Margaret was born her mother experienced a very

painful labour lasting 18 hours. She also received Pethidine injections. Margaret did not suck properly and after a week her mother gave up breastfeeding because she had abcesses. Bottle feeding took an hour and Margaret slept fitfully.

As she grew older she showed other problems. She did not respond to toilet training and was wet in the daytime until four years of age. In fact until the age of five she wet herself unpredictably. She had difficulty in co-ordination and became destructive of her own things and unkind to her brother and sister.

'I asked the Health Visitor to help me with her problems,' her mother told me. 'She called to see me and Margaret walked downstairs with her arms, legs and clothes covered in cold cream! She could see the kind of problem I had, but did not have much advice to give me.'

There seemed to be little advice forthcoming from any source. Her mother was just told that she had a strong-willed child. If she smacked Margaret she fainted, which seemed quite alarming to her mother, but the doctor assured her that she held her breath and caused herself to faint and that there seemed to be no other problem. Margaret lacked the confidence to ask for things in shops and refused to do anything by herself. Visits to friends proved impossible as Margaret refused to allow her mother to dress her. She caused such a fuss that it seemed easier to stay at home. On one occasion, Margaret went into their garden and pulled the heads off all the flowers she could find.

'I felt at a loss to know what to do with her,' says her mother. 'I would lock myself in the toilet and cry and cry because I just could not get through to her.'

One of her friends asked her how she was getting on with Margaret.

'Little children are like animals, aren't they? You have to be strong and firm with them,' she remembers saying. Her friend looked shocked at this, but at the time it seemed to be true to her; she thought that all children were like Margaret.

'It was not until I had my two other babies that I realised that children can really be sweet and nice.'

As Margaret did not settle at play school, nor when she began to attend school regularly, her mother received advice to

see the child psychologist to help her with her daughter's problems. He found nothing wrong except that she was hesitant in making decisions. However at school she showed no improvement and would disrupt the class or daydream, sitting for long periods without working. One of her teachers said of her, 'You think that you are getting through to Margaret and that she is co-operating but suddenly you find that she is not, so you can never get very far with her.'

Someone suggested that they might find help from the Hyperactive Children's Support Group and the food programme. First, Margaret's mother removed orange squash from her diet for one week. She seemed calmer and better to get on with, so her mother put her onto the full diet and soon noticed an improvement. This began during the last six months at primary school. Since starting secondary school she has added the use of Evening Primrose Oil and vitamin tablets. Margaret's behaviour is improving as the benefits from these build up in her system.

Joining the HACSG has helped the whole family, for it brought a general realisation of the effect food can have on daily life. They have improved the quality of food eaten by everyone in the family and have turned to the use of whole foods. They leave out 'junk foods' which are full of sugar, colourings, additives and preservatives and which have very little nutritional value.

Her mother looks for reasons for the change in Margaret's behaviour.

'The change in her diet has obviously helped her a lot. Perhaps psychologically I am more relaxed, too, as I now have support through contact with the group. Also Margaret has moved on to secondary school. The school is excellent and the staff really go out of their way to help their pupils and co-operate with parents. I just hope that, with all this support to hand, Margaret will mature and become a sensible and reliable person.

'People used to say to me, "Of course she will soon be going through a difficult time." I find this amusing,' says her mother, 'as, if anything, she is getting better day by day!'

Sylvia

Following a normal pregnancy and labour, Mrs Robinson gave birth to her second daughter, Sylvia. About an hour before the birth she received a shot of Pethidine and when Sylvia came into the world she took a while to take her first breath and seemed very sleepy for the first three or four days. For the first 24 hours she had to be tube fed. Breastfeeding proved to be rather unsuccessful and her weight gain seemed poor, so Sylvia received supplementary bottles from six weeks onwards. She always seemed restless, did not settle in the evenings until after midnight and then slept poorly. There was a marked contrast with her older sister who had been breastfed until six months and always slept well.

At 10 weeks weaning began and then Sylvia's troubles really started. She had been sleeping for a total of seven or eight hours each night, but now she would wake up for two hours every night; she would scream and nothing would placate her. At 10 months she gave up her daytime sleep but still continued to wake at night. The wakeful hours were now between midnight and two in the morning. She would become very distressed and seemed to be unconsolable. This upset her mother at first, but eventually it made her angry.

Sylvia first began to drink orange squash instead of baby orange at the age of one. She developed a severe nappy rash which put her in hospital for a week. Mrs Robinson did not link the rash with the orange squash until years later, so continued to give her orange squash to drink.

By the time Sylvia reached two years of age her mother desperately needed a rest.

'She was demanding, whining and full of energy and would never sit still to watch television or look at a book.' A place at play school gave them the break from each other which her mother so much needed.

As Sylvia grew a little older her behaviour at home worsened:

'Her play was not really destructive,' says Mrs Robinson, 'but she would quickly lose patience with her toys and throw them across the room. She made friends with other children easily but I was always terrified that she would hurt her sister, two-and-a-half years younger than her, as she was sometimes rather violent and always unpredictable.

'Sylvia was almost impossible to discipline. She was naughty, usually after eating food. Smacking her had no useful effect – she just laughed. Putting her in her room did not work – she merely wrecked it. Reasoning with her failed – she wouldn't listen. She would lie on the floor and "moan" for two or three hours if her bad behaviour was ignored.'

Sylvia's younger sister proved to be an angel in comparison. Her mother thinks that if she had not had her she would have been unable to cope with Sylvia as well as she did. She had lost confidence in her ability as a mother while trying to manage Sylvia, but the third child restored her faith in herself. Later she gave birth to a son, but sadly he died when only 15 weeks old (a cot death). Incidentally she breastfed him but he seemed a wakeful baby and did not appear as if he would be easy to bring up.

'By the time Sylvia reached four-and-a-half years old she was awful!' comments Mrs Robinson. 'We had the four children by then – aged seven, four-and-a-half, two, and the new baby – and never a night's sleep. She woke every night and came in for some pretty rough treatment from me.'

By chance the family changed to eating wholemeal bread and they quickly noticed an improvement in Sylvia. Prior to this her mother had noticed that Aspirin and Phenergan had a bad effect on her, although the doctor found this amusing when she mentioned it. Then the family moved North and suddenly found themselves surrounded by people who were keen on the use of good diets and health foods. One of these friends advised her to take Sylvia to see a local paediatrician.

'He is a great believer in diet and put Sylvia on an elimination programme. Two days later she slept for thirteen hours and has never woken in the night since,' says her delighted mother. 'Her behaviour improved a lot. We slowly reintroduced other foods, but kept her on goat's milk for months until now, two years later, she is on a normal diet except for a few items. She is even able to take orange squash in isolated amounts. Only one particular brand of biscuit now produces a reaction.'

During the two years of trial and error with foods they found that the reactions were mostly of a depressive kind, with tears, many falls and bumps and times when everything went wrong. But throughout this period Sylvia continued to sleep well.

'At seven years old she is quite a normal child – lively and often difficult, but not unmanageable – and she sleeps about ten hours a night. She seems to do all right at school and has many friends,' reports her mother.

'Sylvia has had a lot to cope with in her life – three house moves and a fourth due shortly, the addition of two siblings and then the death of the youngest. It has sometimes been hard to tell whether it is the food or the circumstances that have made her difficult, but I would like to say to other parents who are struggling: Sylvia came through it, we have survived, and hopefully she has come to terms with her food sensitivities. She may have outgrown them or they may recur, but thanks to the help we have received from the paediatrician and the Hyperactive Children's Support Group we shall know how to cope.'

Richard

He is a big boy for his age, seven-and-a-half, and has blond hair and blue eyes. His parents had been hoping for a baby for more than four years before Mrs Lewis became pregnant. When she was three months pregnant she almost had a miscarriage and had to rest for a month; when six-and-a-half months pregnant she had to give up work in order to keep the baby. She had high blood pressure and went into hospital six weeks before the birth.

Richard seemed fine for four or five months but Mrs Lewis remembers that on his first New Year's Eve he screamed from six in the evening until midnight and there seemed nothing she could do to quieten him. Soon after this, when they spent a week with relatives, he cried for hours, seemed hungry all the time and again nothing seemed to quieten him. He had a great many dirty nappies that week, too. The clinic advised Mrs Lewis to find a food that would really satisfy him. His sleeping had by this time become a problem and he began to bang his head on the wall.

By the time Richard reached two-and-a-half years of age Mrs Lewis had become pregnant again. She experienced similar

difficulties with this pregnancy, but had to go to hospital more often for rest. This obviously upset the little boy, and after her first absence of a week he would not come near her when she returned, and later tried to kick her and hit her in the stomach. Then he began throwing himself at the furniture and needed watching all the time in case he injured himself. Soon after this he had an accident in the family car, when he took it over for a few minutes! His parents left him sitting very securely fastened in his car seat while they walked to a front door to collect a rocking horse. He somehow managed to climb out of his seat, got into the front of the car, let off the handbrake and pulled the car out of gear. It ran forward and collided with other parked cars. The whole thing happened while his parents were within sight of the car and within two minutes of their getting out of it.

A doctor at the clinic told Mrs Lewis that Richard was hyperactive but that he would grow out of it. He suggested that the little boy go to a play group. They took his advice, but there were problems there, too. He spent a lot of time climbing about and one day came home with a black eye sustained when he fell off a book shelf.

'Things were getting bad generally, so I went to the doctor again,' says his mother. 'He sent us to see the child psychologist. After many visits and many questions I came away feeling that the problems were my fault.'

His mother thought that a change of play group might help, but it did not. Richard ran around all the time, never sat still to listen to the stories, broke the puzzles and became generally destructive.

'None of the children in our street would play with him either. I had a succession of mothers knocking on my door telling me what Richard had done to their children,' his mother remembers.

Richard could not accompany his parents on shopping trips as he rearranged all the shelves in the shop, and he made life very difficult for them when away from home. At the age of four-and-a-half the family took him to a holiday camp. They thought he would enjoy himself in the nursery there, but he opened the safety lock on the nursery gate and let all the children out, so his presence was not required again.

'I felt really low by the time Richard began school,' says Mrs Lewis. 'The problems got worse there, but we had a very good understanding with the headmistress and his own teacher. They got us a lot of help and were very good with Richard.'

At the school Richard began stealing and continued to be destructive and restless. Each day when his mother went to collect him she found that he had taken off nearly all his clothes. She had to spend time dressing him before they could leave for home. The educational psychologist tested him at school and told his parents that he had an above average IQ and was in fact a bright child.

'One day I found Richard on his bedroom window ledge trying to see if he could fly. When I talked him back into the room his eyes were glazed and he didn't seem to know what he was doing,' remembers his mother. 'Another time he set off to play with a friend but instead walked all the way back to his school to a lamp post which had been vandalised. He had taken a pair of wire cutters from the shed and he tried to repair the light. We did not know where he had been until a policeman

came to our door asking if the wire cutters were ours. This type of thing worried and confused us.'

The rest of the family were prompt to tell Mr and Mrs Lewis that they were going the wrong way about bringing up Richard. They could not understand why he should be so difficult. Friends and relations began to visit less and less frequently. Then, about 12 months ago, Mrs Lewis joined a local group giving help to parents of hyperactive children. As a result she found that Richard could not tolerate beet sugar, wheat and yeast.

'Since then we have been paying regular visits to the allergy clinic at our local hospital. Out of 15 tests done he is clear on only two,' says his mother. 'He has drops for things he reacts to and extra vitamins and he is a lot better. We still have bad days but more and more good days. His teacher reports that she is very pleased with his work now and says that he seems to be able to concentrate much better than he did six months ago.'

I met Mrs Lewis again recently and she told me that they had just had a holiday in Italy. She noticed that there Richard was fine. On enquiring she found that the country only allows a couple of artificial colours to be used – the rest are banned. How long will it take to ban artificial colours in this country, I wonder?

Alex
At the tender age of five weeks little Alex moved in to live with a family not his by birth. His parents knew nothing of his birth when they adopted him, but they say that he appeared to be a good baby, although he tended to bring up his feeds.

When Alex reached one year he began to have excessive fixations for curtains and stairs. He had tantrums if not allowed to play with them, his mother remembers. He slept very little. This reached a peak at the age of 22 months when he would not settle or even stay in bed until 11 or later at night and woke again around two in the morning. His parents were lucky if he had half an hour's sleep during the rest of the night. His mother also noticed that he walked very clumsily and she sought help from the doctor. He examined Alex and asked his mother to account for every bruise.

'You can imagine how I felt,' says his mother.

The whole matter came to a head when his mother became ill and had to be rushed into hospital. Grandmother took over but failed to cope with Alex because he threw things around and had tantrums. His father took him to his own doctor who diagnosed hyperactivity and prescribed Valium. Everyone in the family was appalled by this, but his mother felt greatly relieved that someone had acknowledged the problem. He continued to take Valium until the age of five when he began attending a diagnostic unit, and he moved on to a remedial school at the age of seven. His mother explains that he is not really a child needing remedial help but that he could not cope in a normal school because of his unacceptable behaviour and unsociable ways. He is in fact a bright child with an average IQ. From four years of age his drug programme included Ritalin to help his concentration during the day, Mogadon (adult dosage) and Tofranyl at night, as well as Valium occasionally. He went into a children's hospital for three weeks to try to balance and control his drugs but the hospital were unable to cope with him. Later Valium and Mogadon were withdrawn.

At six years of age Alex began the Feingold food programme and his reading age rose from under five to seven in six months. His behaviour at school improved noticeably, too. As a younger child he had been very aggressive, biting, pinching, and pulling hair. His mother notices that this is much less of a problem now that he is older. At the age of nine he still takes Ritalin. His parents took him off it for a while but he had to go back onto it because of behaviour problems.

'Now it is mainly a social problem. He asks silly questions. He is annoying at times and likes to wind other people up. He can be very disruptive sometimes,' says his mother. 'He is ready to sleep at night now but wakes up between five and six in the morning. His concentration is good if he is interested in the subject, but otherwise it is poor. His co-ordination is a little better but his writing is still very bad and he has difficulty with maths.'

Alex has a social worker who visits him. His present doctor is very sympathetic but sceptical about the value of his food programme although he prescribes Efavite and Efamol (see p. 181). Alex has no brothers or sisters as his parents were advised that he would not be able to cope with the competition. His parents see a great improvement in him as they look back over the years; even the problem of bedwetting, which has continued until the present, is showing signs of improvement. His parents find that he responds to behaviour modification techniques better than to a spanking. At school there are 'team points' as a reward and his parents carry this on at home too. He can save up points which he has gained for good behaviour to obtain toys, books, or other things that he particularly wants.

His mother is a Contact for the HACSG. Other parents phone her but they are too widely spread to get together for meetings. The Citizens' Advice Bureau also ring her with enquiries. She has spoken on the radio, too.

In conclusion Alex's mother says:

'I think all mothers go through a self-doubting situation and probably a period of depression. At such times a sympathetic doctor is essential. I became a Contact as I felt so cut off from society. I didn't visit anyone, didn't like to take Alex shopping, or anything like that.

'Alex has been quite a happy chap throughout. He now gets very upset when reprimanded over certain things but I honestly don't think that he can help it.'

Jeremy

Elizabeth gave birth to a baby boy following a normal pregnancy but a long labour of 28 hours. Jeremy weighed seven-and-a-half pounds and had slight jaundice at birth, but was otherwise fine. His mother breastfed him, but on return from the hospital he screamed a great deal, seemed to suffer from colic and did not sleep very much. His sleeping did not improve, nor did the colic, and he always seemed very tense, twitching in his sleep and waking at the slightest sound. He often screamed as if in severe pain and pushed away from his mother so that she found it difficult to hold him.

'As he grew a little older he did not smile as other children seemed to do, but he was my first child so I didn't realise that he was much different from other babies,' remembers his mother. 'I used to drive him around in the car to stop him crying as it seemed to soothe him.'

As a toddler he seemed to be in perpetual motion. Elizabeth

walked the parks with him for hours as she found it easier to be out than at home where he stripped the wallpaper and touched everything in sight. It seemed to her that he grizzled the whole time. He never played with toys as did other children of his age but had an obsession with wheels and would sit quietly for long periods watching a wheel go round. He spoke little until two years of age when he suddenly came out with quite a complicated sentence. From an early age Elizabeth noticed that he became much worse after eating sweets or 'instant whips', so she cut them out of his diet before he reached three years.

'I felt absolutely desperate and depressed and didn't know where to turn, knowing that something was wrong but not what,' says Elizabeth. 'I was a single parent – I think if I'd had a husband I'd never have coped at all as I neglected everything and devoted my life to romping all over the place with my son. I was worried about going to the doctor as I thought he'd probably think it was me not coping as a single parent – but I knew it wasn't me. In the end I did go and tell him that Jeremy didn't sleep and he gave me Phenobarb for him, which didn't help, but I never told him the real problem.'

Jeremy's father has various psychiatric problems, Elizabeth told me. He is obsessional and was diagnosed as manic depressive. Elizabeth and Jeremy have no contact with him now.

An article by Sally Bunday in a magazine caught Elizabeth's eye. It told of the Feingold food programme and she felt sufficiently impressed to try it with Jeremy.

'Within three days he slept throughout the night, his nightmares stopped, his aggression diminished, he smiled at me and let me hold him. His whole personality changed. It was so wonderful that I just couldn't believe it. He has been on the programme ever since. His behaviour reverts if he goes off it. He is now eleven and a bright boy at school with plenty of friends and interests.'

Elizabeth felt so overjoyed by the complete change in her son that she volunteered to be a contact for the HACSG. Meetings of the Group are also held every other month in a nearby town, when parents living near Elizabeth meet with the group there.

Norman

Until Norman was three he had no real problems. He began nursery school but always seemed to be in trouble as he lacked concentration, was disruptive and aggressive and could not play. At five-and-a-half years of age he went to infant school where he experienced the same problems and so spent more time outside the classroom door than inside the room. Frequent visits by his mother to the headmistress failed to resolve anything.

A suggestion was made that Norman might benefit from a smaller class with more attention from the teacher. Although he had abundant language and asked endless questions, at the age of seven he had only just begun to read. He moved to a small unit which at first seemed ideal for him. However he still had numerous problems and the teacher suggested that his mother try putting him on the Feingold food programme.

'By then I was prepared to try anything,' says his mother. 'We started the diet and friends soon began to notice a difference in Norman, but his weight and a lack of vitamins worried me. I took him to the doctor for ideas but he told me that he knew nothing about such diets and referred us to our local hospital. The consultant there did not believe in food sensitivity and related problems. When I mentioned that we had started Norman on Oil of Evening Primrose and it seemed to work well, he told us that we might as well give him corn oil.'

They went back in three months. Norman's behaviour had stabilised on the diet, he had returned to his previous school and could cope fairly well there, but he did not gain weight. The consultant suggested that they admit Norman to hospital for observation for one week to do some tests.

'Great, I thought. Maybe we can at last get some help for Norman.'

Norman went into hospital and straight away he received food not recommended on the Feingold food programme.

'He was noisy, rude, and climbed up the curtains,' his mother told me, 'but we did not try to stop him during visits as he was there for observation. By the end of the week we could stand the destruction no more. We knew it would take some time to get him right again and it had achieved nothing. We took him home and began to undo the damage.

'I don't know if Norman is typical of hyperactive children. I only know that in three years of trials, certain foods do affect his behaviour; of this I am convinced. If parents can find a doctor who believes this, then they are very lucky. After three years of trying in our area I am about ready to give up. I am a mere mother with no qualifications and I am constantly asked by medical people, "What would you like us to do?"'

Robin

There are two boys in the Eastwood family. Robin is eight years old, three years older than his brother. Although Robin's birth had no complications, he had problems in abundance from then on. For three months he suffered from colic, he cried incessantly, had feeding problems, and later became accident prone; he had poor balance, was extremely clumsy, had poor eye and hand co-ordination (he could not hold a pencil properly until over five years of age), fidgeted constantly, touched everything, had poor concentration, was impulsive, had poor tolerance of frustration, tending to over react to everything in an excitable manner, had tantrums and a delay in language development.

Under these circumstances, Joan Eastwood, his mother, gratefully accepted help from her mother who cared for Robin every Saturday morning in order to give her a break. The other grandmother tended to think that Robin would benefit from a good hiding. Most other relatives were quite understanding and sympathetic.

'One quickly learns in such situations who are one's real friends,' comments Joan. 'Very often I found it was the people whom I thought would give sympathetic help who didn't and assistance tended to come from the least expected sources.'

The teachers at Robin's school proved to be very understanding, in particular the reception teacher. The health visitor also meant well, Joan thinks, but the whole situation seemed to be beyond her experience. Robin saw various doctors at the group practice. They were mostly helpful and referred him to specialists, but either they did not recognise that he was hyperactive or did not tell his mother what they thought. Nothing happened about his speech difficulty for six years, until a new doctor joined the practice.

'He immediately realised that the problem was not due to bad upbringing but to "minimal cerebral dysfunction". He consulted the speech therapist and ever since he has bent over backwards to help in every way possible,' says Joan. Through tests it came to light that Robin had an allergy to cow's milk. He also went onto the Feingold food programme.

Robin had some problems at school. His delayed language development seemed to be the main trouble. He went into a remedial class initially but once he became established on the Feingold programme most of his educational difficulties disappeared. He then made such rapid progress that he caught up with his peers.

Looking back his parents remember that Robin's problems were a great burden to them.

'We regarded him as a constant source of worry, not knowing why he was different. It was a problem that would never leave us; it was there twenty-four hours a day. Of course, the main problem is that it is a hidden handicap. Hyperactive children look so normal. I always thought that if there was something really wrong with Robin it would have been discovered almost immediately after his birth. Also, being my first child, I had no one with whom to compare him.

'My biggest regret is that I did not get to know about the Hyperactive Children's Support Group earlier, because the food programme has worked miracles for my son. I am now able to lead a life of my own, too, instead of constantly having to see to his needs,' rejoices his mother.

'Dealing with a hyperactive child is an experience which no one can begin to comprehend unless they have had experience of it for twenty-four hours a day. Unfortunately, many social workers, health visitors and those who become involved with these children have not even had experience of bringing up "normal" children. Obviously this cannot be helped, but I do think that the "experts" spend too much time scrutinising the mother instead of having a good look at the child.'

Terry

This little lad is the first and, they maintain, the last child of Mr and Mrs Lovell.

'I haven't the desire to go through all that again,' says his mother. 'It was too traumatic. My husband and I have fully recovered from the ordeal and family life is happy at last, but it has taken several years to get to this stage. It seems like a lifetime – and it *is* a lifetime for Terry.'

During her pregnancy, Mrs Lovell had sickness for the full nine months with heartburn for the last 10 weeks. She had numerous scans and one X-ray during the last 10 weeks of pregnancy. Labour lasted 18 hours and she received three doses of Pethidine and two epidurals. Terry was delivered by forceps while his mother was under general anaesthetic.

During the first few days of his life she had very little contact with Terry, for the epidurals left her paralysed for seven days. The standard of nursing care seemed poor and as she could not get to her baby she could not see much of him. Later they moved to a nursing home where they had every chance to be together, but he did not seem to want her. The only time he stopped screaming and appeared relaxed and happy was when he lay in his cot in a room of his own. His mother began to fear that he might be autistic, but there were so many day-to-day health problems at the time, as well as the fact that she felt she had made an awful fuss about the birth, that she did not dare mention autism to the doctor. Her fears regarding this gradually diminished during the first year of Terry's life.

When Terry reached 17 months Mrs Lovell took him to the doctor because he had been unable to sleep for three weeks. He would often play throughout the night, and although he occasionally slept for one hour during the day, he often fought sleep for up to 24 hours. The doctor told her that she would have to learn to cope. During the next six months she visited the doctor and health visitor regularly with the same problem. They told her that she was an incompetent mother. In the beginning she fought their opinion but as the months passed she began to believe them and almost had a nervous breakdown. Her own family lived many miles away and only saw Terry for very short periods. Their advice to her was 'Pull yourself together'. The marriage suffered badly, and because Terry's behaviour had become so unsociable, she stopped seeing other mothers with young children. She felt completely isolated with all her problems. The few friends she did see assured her that Terry was quite normal. She thinks that they were trying to be kind, but at the time it made her feel even more inadequate, that she could not cope with a normal child.

During the summer months before Terry reached two years of age, his mother remembers him as aggressive and generally uncontrollable. He suffered from travel sickness on even the very shortest of trips, demanded company to play with him through the night and banged his head on the concrete path. His mother became almost afraid to be left alone with him because she could not control him. In the Autumn they put him onto a wholefood diet. A few days later he became worse and did not appear to know his parents. Later they found that this happened because they had withdrawn food from his diet to which he was sensitive and he was suffering withdrawal symptoms. In a day or two he was playing happily with a box of bricks and then slept for three hours during the morning. That night he slept for 14 hours; his parents could hardly believe it. That week he became very affectionate and enjoyed sitting on his mother's lap for as long as an hour. The thirst he had always suffered subsided.

Mrs Lovell keeps a case history of Terry which she updates every six months. After the initial problem had been solved, whenever he was difficult she would note all the symptoms and what she later discovered had caused them. She found that tap water made him hyperactive at one stage. The use of bottled water solved another problem, too: he ceased to wet the bed. Looking back, Mrs Lovell realised that, as a small child, he had always screamed and been very badly behaved after he had been swimming. At the time she had just thought that he did not like the changing area.

Then she noticed that he was sensitive to cheese, cottage cheese and yoghurt. She heard that the rennet in these contains salicylate and this is something that seems to cause trouble with children liable to be hyperactive.

Terry started a course of Efamol (see p. 181). His mother also had his hair and finger nails analysed as advised by Foresight (see p. 235). As a result of these tests he began a course of dietary supplements and treatment to get rid of the lead in his body, as both tests showed high readings of lead. He has also had homeopathic treatment which has meant that his diet can now be more varied. He follows a rotation diet so that he is not eating the same food too often, as he develops intolerances to food which he eats too frequently.

Mrs Lovell became a group leader for the Hyperactive Children's Support Group in her area.

'We hold meetings once a month. This gives the parents the opportunity to talk about their practical, social and emotional problems associated with caring for a hyperactive child. We exchange recipes, lend books and have discussions on medical matters. A lot of the parents have turned to homeopathy, as so often doctors prescribe medicines which have sugar and colourings in them. These are not suitable for hyperactive children in a lot of cases.'

Gordon

Some time ago I spoke to Gordon's mother and she told me that she would be willing to share her experiences with me, choosing to write rather than talk about the problems caused by her son's hyperactivity. Eventually I heard from her and she explained the reason for the delay in contacting me.

'I tried on numerous occasions to make notes. I found it very difficult to do, probably because of the length of time involved (my son is now 14), but mainly because I found the whole process very painful. Deep down I don't want to remember. Writing made me recall the pain, frustration, depression and loneliness my husband and I felt for 12 years. We had no help from anyone.'

Her reply is therefore very meaningful, as it is wrung from the anguish of her years of despair. It sums up the problems often experienced by parents who have this problem to deal with day in, day out. The added frustration of being told that there is nothing wrong with a child, and worse still, that the parents are the cause of any visible problems when they are doing all they can to aid the child, is extremely difficult to bear.

Gordon's mother outlined his early days. She said that she tried to breastfeed him for three days after his birth but he would not suck properly. A nurse in the hospital suggested that his mother give him some cereal with his night feed as she thought that it might keep him quiet. He could not take it, and vomited it back. On the tenth day after his birth they left hospital with a parting remark from the hospital staff: 'You will have trouble with that one!'

During the first few months at home his mother found it very difficult to organise any kind of routine. Gordon cried constantly and vomited most of his feeds. He slept for only about 10 or 15 minutes every two hours or so. His mother took him for regular checks and he appeared to be quite normal. When she mentioned the crying they remarked, 'ALL babies cry, Mrs Charlton.'

His parents only found real peace when they drove him around in the car.

'We did a lot of driving in the first three months!' remarked his mother.

As he grew a little older the problems continued. He refused any drinks in the night and his mother stopped trying to comfort him when he cried as he went rigid if she attempted to cuddle him.

'I felt rejection and anger and thought it better for all concerned if I touched him only when necessary, such as at feed times and when I changed him.'

At six months Gordon became very active and crawled around, but still would not sleep. When playing on the floor he would suddenly scream and sometimes vomit. The doctor put this down to teething, and sure enough, at seven months he cut six teeth in one week. His parents hoped for a little peace after this but he still did not sleep, although they kept him awake all day in the hope that he would be tired at night. They had to sleep in shifts in order to care for him, rather than both be disturbed all night.

At 10 months he began to sleep a little better, for five hours at a time. He chose to sleep during the evening, however, and no matter how they tried, his parents could not move those hours so that they coincided with the rest of the household's sleeping hours. There was one benefit, however. They could have a baby sitter in now and again and go out for the evening, which helped them to relax a little. Gordon walked at 11 months. At this age his mother described him thus:

'A miserable and unhappy child with miserable and unhappy parents desperate for peace and quiet. Before he reached his first birthday Gordon was on sleeping drugs and I took tranquillisers, neither of which worked. We felt trapped and desperate.'

Gordon's sleeping pattern finally altered when he reached 18 months. He slept from eight at night until eight in the morning and then woke with great difficulty. He still remained a problem, however, as he had a short temper and seemed to be a nervous child not able to cope with groups of children.

On Gordon's second day at school, he had a fight with the headmistress. He always held intelligent conversations which tended to unnerve adults and people described him as having 'an old head on young shoulders'. He would not put up with other people's foolish remarks. The main complaint from his teachers was that he talked all the time, never kept still and did very untidy work. Everyone recognised that he needed firm discipline.

'Outings always ended in disaster with Gordon in a temper or a black mood. He hardly ever smiled and had no sense of humour, finding no fun in anything,' remembers his mother.

The only thing that held his interest over the years proved to be horse riding. He began riding at nine years of age and still rides at 14 and has a pony of his own. He could not maintain his concentration on other things. From the age of 10 his aggression became worse with more physical violence. His temper became unpredictable: he would suddenly flare up for no logical reason and then remain moody for days afterwards. As he neared 12 his parents wondered how they could cope with him and keep him under control. Would he turn into a juvenile delinquent as he grew physically bigger and stronger?

An article by Sally Bunday of the Hyperactive Children's Support Group came into Mrs Charlton's hands. A description in it seemed to fit Gordon so accurately in certain respects that she sent for the food programme. She tried him on it, not really believing that it would do very much to help him.

'Within five days Gordon had changed. He became calmer and more relaxed and things which would have sparked his temper just seemed to wash over him. Friends who met him remarked that he looked different, with no bags under his eyes, and his skin looked a better colour.

'During the first two weeks of the programme he lost his temper once, but came back after five minutes and said

"Sorry" for the first time ever, and put his arms around me. I cried,' says his mother.

As Mrs Charlton looks back she sees his childhood as a time of misery, nervousness, temper tantrums and moods which have affected the whole family. They found no professional help or understanding and felt cheated out of enjoying their first child. They could give each other no happiness and his parents felt let down.

'At 14 years old he still occasionally loses his temper but quickly recovers. He has turned into quite a comic during the last two years, with a dry sense of humour. He still has some difficulty in concentrating for long periods of time, but the frightening aggression and tension have gone. He is turning into an amiable young man.

'Of course some of these things may be due to his getting older and maturing, but the dramatic change two years ago could only be due to his change of diet,' concludes his mother.

The foregoing pages have described how parents have tried to help and cope with their hyperactive children. But what are the views of the experts? Do they recognise the problems that parents and children face? Do they offer any reasons for them? If so, what do they recommend? The third part of this book is devoted to an investigation into the ways of helping such children and the views of those in a position to assist them.

PART THREE
Professional Views on Hyperactivity

Introduction:
Where Can We Find Help?

A child who is hyperactive is difficult to cope with at any time, but some parents soldier on, day in, day out, year after year. However there are times when most parents of a hyperactive child find it very difficult to manage. They may have succeeded in coping with the problems when the child was small, perhaps at the cost of their social life and a total rearrangement of their sleeping habits and daily life, but then suddenly something new or unexpected may happen which upsets their carefully laid plans. Ill health of either parent, additional problems presented by the child (or merely the same old problems grinding away until breaking point is reached), a change of house or parent's job, the arrival or expected arrival of a new baby, problems with the child at the play group or with his education; any one of a multitude of additional problems can unbalance the routine which the parents have established. On the other hand, the parents may reach the point where they are not prepared to watch an apparently normal child behave in such a strange way and dominate their lives. They would prefer to find out the reason why their child is 'odd' and do something to help him live in a normally accepted way for a child of his age. Why allow him to suffer, and why suffer along with him, when perhaps something can be done to clear up the problem?

Having made the decision to find help, where do they look? The first person whom most parents turn to is their doctor. This may prove to be helpful or it may do no good whatsoever. It depends on whether the particular doctor has had any contact with the problem previously and what his views are on the subject. He may be extremely helpful and suggest treatment himself or recommend that they see a paediatrician at a local hospital. It is possible that he may prescribe drugs to lessen the problem, or he may suggest that visits to the local child guidance clinic will be helpful. He may recommend that the parents contact the Hyperactive Children's Support Group. On the other hand he may have preconceived ideas about the problems of such children and have come to the conclusion that such behaviour in the child is the result of the parent's neurotic state of mind. In that case he might treat the mother with a sedative to help her relax, assuming that the child will then recover.

There are a growing number of doctors who are not prepared to look merely at the symptoms which their patients present. They look for the cause behind the symptoms and one suggested cause is that some hyperactive children have a sensitivity to certain foods which bring about a variety of symptoms. Rather than treating the symptoms with drug therapy or referring the child to someone who specialises in the behavioural approach to the problems, they consider the possibility that the child may not be able to tolerate certain foods in his diet. As a result of this he exhibits physical symptoms and mental disturbances.

We are all familiar with hay-fever and are used to hearing the pollen count read daily. We accept that a hay-fever sufferer has physical problems because he comes into contact with something that his body cannot tolerate. As we are constantly taking food and air into our bodies, it is logical to suggest that, possibly, not everything we like has the same regard for us as we have for it. In the United States of America there are hundreds of allergy clinics. In Britain there are perhaps less than a dozen clinics where one can go for help and little or no treatment is available under the National Health Service.

Food sensitivities can be very difficult to track down. When a person eats something regularly which his body cannot handle effectively, he may feel fine for a while before he begins to see his usual problems occurring. This is known as masking. If he ceases to eat that particular food regularly, he will at first feel worse and then gradually recover. This can clearly be seen in the case of alcohol. The immediate effect of alcoholic drink is that of elation. It is later that the other symptoms begin – and a hangover often prompts the person to take another drink, as this then relieves the symptoms for a while.

According to the specialists in this field, some people may be sensitive to a large number of different things. If all of these cannot be traced and the person is in regular contact with them, then the symptoms will not clear up. They may reduce slightly but it is something like having several nails sticking up in a shoe. Remove one or two nails and the wearer notices an improvement but is not fully content until all the offending nails are removed.

Dr T. G. Randolph and his co-author, R. W. Moss, in their book *Allergies – Your Hidden Enemy*, have the following dedication:

> This book is dedicated to all patients who have ever been called neurotic, hypochondriac, hysterical, or starved for attention, while actually suffering from environmentally induced illness.

In the chapter entitled 'Hidden Addictions' we read:

> Of course some people do know that they are allergic to certain foods, but in general these are foods that are rarely eaten. A person who is allergic to cashews, for instance, may break out in a rash on the rare occasion when he consumes these nuts. He overcomes this problem by simply avoiding cashews, and that is generally the end of the matter.
>
> Allergies to commonly eaten foods are not readily detected or avoided, however. Let us say, for instance, that you develop an allergy to milk early in life. At first, this may have resulted in acute reactions, such as a rash or a cough. In time, if the allergy was not recognised and controlled, the symptoms may have become generalized and less easily detected. Since you probably went on drinking milk or eating milk products almost every day, one day's symptons blurred into the next day's. You developed a chronic disease, such as arthritis, migraine, or depression. It never occurred to you that your daily dose of milk was the source of the problem.
>
> In fact, you were probably abusing milk. You had become a milk junkie, a milk-o-holic. It is in the nature of this problem that a sudden loss of the craved substance can cause withdrawal symptoms. Since removal of milk brought on a

particularly bad attack of the symptoms, you unconsciously learned to keep yourself on a maintenance dose. Milk in the morning with cereal, milk in your coffee, yoghurt for lunch, a glass of milk with your dinner, and, of course a platter of cheese tidbits before retiring. (p. 16)

Later in his book there are case histories of extreme difficulties with hyperactive children whose problems were solved by finding and eliminating the food or environmental conditions which did not suit them.

There is a great deal of suspicion in medical circles regarding food allergies. Many people who themselves have problems, or who have problem children, also find it hard at first to believe that food can make any difference to behaviour and tend to think that it is just a way of excusing bad behaviour. I myself tended to need convincing, but see much more relevance now than when I first began to look into the subject. Seeing how well many hyperactive children have responded to various diet treatments I cannot but recommend any other parents with the problem in their family to give serious thought to the subject and to put it to the test for themselves.

11 The Hyperactive Children's Support Group

The Hyperactive Children's Support Group (HACSG) has been referred to on a number of occasions throughout this book. For many parents it has proved to be the only life-line available to them in their difficulties when coping with a hyperactive or very difficult child. I did not know of its existence until a year or so ago, and by then my daughter's problems had decreased. Not all parents are as fortunate as we have been. Despite the severe behaviour problems with which we had to cope and the problems with education, Tanya slept well at night (given the right circumstances for actually going to sleep in the first place) and she has grown out of the problem, something which does not happen to all children.

The Hyperactive Children's Support Group came into being in 1977 through the initiative of one mother whose child . was offered drugs as a remedy for his hyperactivity. She began searching for alternatives and, having achieved encouraging results by putting him on a food programme which eliminated chemical additives – colouring, flavouring and preservatives – she began to tell others about it. Almost overnight she had an overwhelming response and the HACSG was born, much to her dismay. As a mother who also went out to work for a large part of the week, Sally Bunday could barely keep pace with the demands on her time and energy. She had to change her telephone number and go ex-directory in order to stop the telephone ringing day and night, and every day the postman delivered piles of letters. Since then she has accomplished a mammoth task: running the Group, organising conferences, fulfilling speaking engagements, writing endless letters, contacting doctors, politicians, researchers, even the Prime Minister, to mention just a few, as well as collecting information and passing it on via newsletters which are sent to members at regular intervals.

She is assisted in her work by her mother, Mrs I. D. Colquhoun, who is Honorary Chairman of the Group, but over the last few years little outside help has been available because the work is done from their respective homes and there has been no money to rent an office and pay for a secretary. Considering how much has been accomplished under such difficult circumstances, how much more could have been done had Sally been free to work full time for the Group, with a secretary to handle all the correspondence from an office.

The Support Group recommends a food programme researched by the late Dr Ben Feingold MD, an American allergist. For a small fee parents join the group and receive a copy of the recommended diet and regular copies of the Newsletter. They can also receive individual help, if necessary, from either Sally Bunday or Mrs Colquhoun, and can be put in touch with a doctor who will help. The food programme, 'anglicised' by Sally from Dr Feingold's work, is fairly easy to follow but, she insists, needs perseverance. Two groups of foods are eliminated by the diet – fruit and vegetables containing natural salicylates, to which some children show sensitivity, and food and drink which contains synthetic colouring, flavouring and preservatives. Instructions on how to carry out the programme are provided for parents to follow. The local support groups form a back-up for parents with children on the diet. The list of 'safe' foods is added to or altered in the Newsletter if changes occur as a result of manufacturers' modifications.

Through the HACSG parents can receive advice and support as soon as the problems are encountered. No longer do they need to suffer alone, feeling helpless and like lepers in the community, because no one can stand their child's behaviour. No longer must they search for answers alone, for many of these can be supplied by the Group. The network of local groups throughout the country, run by parents, provides the opportunity for ideas and problems to be shared. They are able, too, to contact other parents (who do not run groups but act as 'contacts' for the Group) if they wish to share the worst

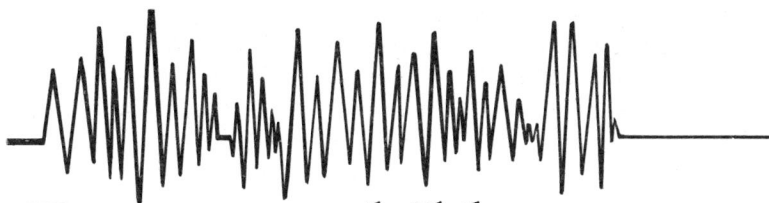

Does your child drive you crazy?

with excessive crying screaming disruptive and aggressive behaviour?

Is your child having problems with sleeping speaking co-ordination & concentration?

If so he or she may be Hyperactive.

The **Hyperactive Childrens Support Group** exists to help you.

Contact us now.

Sally Bunday
59 Meadowside
Angmering
Sussex BN16 4BW

Your local contact is

stories of their child's behaviour with an understanding person. It is surprising how one can actually laugh at a child's awful misdeed when the tale is retold, dissolving the bitterness, anger and frustration in not knowing where to turn. Parents may continue to attend group meetings run by other members or may start their own group. One group which I attend has become a 'Helpline'. Parents with children who are hyperactive or who have severe allergy problems, or who are causing their parents much worry and anxiety, can telephone for help and attend monthly meetings which are addressed by educational psychologists, dieticians, doctors, and other people with information to impart which will help parents to cope.

Incidentally, it is interesting to see that very few men attend the meetings, although occasionally a husband may come with his wife (perhaps the other husbands are all at home coping with the children). Moreover, all those I have spoken to regarding the problems of their children have been women. Husbands are mentioned to me now and then, particularly those who have been prepared to do 'shift work' by staying up for several hours a night to care for a sleepless child, while the mother has some much needed rest. A psychologist also remarked on the fact that at a meeting he held to discuss problems presented by children, there was only one man present, other than himself, amongst a very large audience of women. It might seem to imply that the mother bears the brunt of the problem, occasionally also having to deal with a disgruntled husband who complains about her handling of the child. Some fathers cannot cope with the situation, I am told, and leave the wife to carry on as best she may. I have not actually heard of any mothers leaving specifically because of a hyperactive child, but I should not be surprised if some have at least contemplated running away from their difficulties. I often wished that I could be anywhere but where I was: isolated at home with a problem which would not go away but instead grew bigger and more demanding day by day.

Dr Feingold's hypothesis on the sensitivity of some children to artificial colour, flavour and preservatives has surprisingly been challenged by many people, including C. Keith Conners in a book-length work, *Food Additives and Hyperactive Children*. This challenge has since been carefully considered by

Dr Vicky Rippere and published in the *British Journal of Clinical Psychology* (1983). She contends that the way in which Conners conducted his tests is open to criticism and that he in fact only tested one small area of the diet. It is premature to say that the diet does not work on the basis of the tests he did and she outlines recommendations for further research into the subject.

In his book *Help for the Hyperactive Child*, Dr Sydney Walker also criticises Dr Feingold's book, *Why Your Child is Hyperactive*. He is concerned that the publication of the book provided a way for parents to diagnose and treat their own children. He does not disagree with Dr Feingold's purpose in presenting his views but with the wisdom of bypassing normal medical procedure, which may lead to parents and children struggling to follow the diet prior to receiving a thorough medical examination. If the child has already received the best examination possible and no other causes have been discovered, Dr Walker says that then he would be happy for parents to try eliminating certain items from their child's diet, as they then have nothing to lose. Symptoms of hyperactivity can arise from so many disorders or deficiencies that he cannot conclude that just one kind of treatment (namely the Feingold diet) can be effective for all.

One case that Dr Walker quotes is that of a girl of seven who showed general inability to keep still at home and in school and had sleeping problems. She had been on the drug Ritalin but had shown little improvement and it was discontinued when she began to show side effects of the drug. A diet eliminating all food additives failed to help and a general physical examination revealed nothing abnormal. Finally, after various other examinations, tests revealed that she had pin-worm infestation. When this problem cleared up after treatment, her behaviour improved.

Dr Walker maintains that it could be easy for a child to be labelled as hyperactive while in fact he is suffering from either poisoning of some kind, problems left from an earlier illness, defects or deficiencies, psychiatric problems or any one of a number of serious disorders. He thinks that if some children are treated only by their parents, using the Feingold diet, serious medical problems could easily be overlooked and at worst the child could die through neglect of the correct treatment for the true problem.

The use of drugs for the hyperactive child is not recommended either by Dr Walker. It has been common practice in America for children showing signs of hyperactivity to be put on behaviour altering drugs. I understand that some schools refuse to accept disruptive and overactive children unless they are regularly given drugs. Dr Walker sees drugs merely as a mask for behaviour, not a cure. He warns of the dangers to the children of such drugs because of the side effects of their use, particularly in the long term.

Mrs Colquhoun of the HACSG adds these comments:

> The Feingold diet is not a treatment in the strictest sense. It is simply a change of eating habits. We are, after all, pressed on all sides, from the Department of Health to the health food shops, to improve our eating habits. This is what we are trying to suggest to mothers. We go further than Dr Feingold did in that we try to get mothers to use wholemeal flour, natural sugar and so on, and we also cut out nitrates and nitrites, monosodium glutamate and so on, which Dr Feingold did not do.
>
> Of course we agree that children should have thorough medical examinations, not necessarily based on psychological criteria, for all medical symptoms need taking into consideration; but while a mother is waiting for all that to happen, there is no harm whatsoever in trying the Feingold Food Programme. Dr Feingold endeavoured to get children better without causing them further harm from drugs.
>
> The figure for improvement on the Feingold programme is only about 50%, so we have undertaken research to try to improve the betterment rate.

The Hyperactive Children's Support Group does not limit itself to the Feingold diet alone. It is interested in the problems of lead pollution and has also commissioned research into a lack of essential fatty acids as a possible cause of hyperactivity. As a result of detailed surveys carried out, the Group came to the conclusion that many of the children may have a deficiency of essential fatty acids (EFAs), for various reasons.

The main pieces of evidence are:

1   Most of the food constituents which cause trouble in these children are weak inhibitors of the conversion of EFAs to prostaglandins (PGs).

2   Boys are much more commonly affected than girls and males are known to have much higher requirements for EFAs than females.

3   A high proportion of our children have abnormal thirst, and thirst is one of the cardinal signs of EFA deficiency.

4   Many of our children have eczema, allergies and asthma which some reports suggest can be alleviated by EFAs.

5   Many of our children are deficient in zinc which is required for conversion of EFAs to PGs.

6   Some of our children are badly affected by wheat and milk which are known to give rise to exorphins in the gut which can block conversion of EFAs to PGE1. A preliminary study of EFA supplementation in a number of our children has given promising results. We hope that others with better facilities will be encouraged to test out this hypothesis.* (*Medical Hypothesis 7*: 673–678. 1981, 'A lack of essential fatty acids as a possible cause of hyperactivity in children' – Irene Colquhoun and Sally Bunday, Hyperactive Children's Support Group. Findings from 1979 Survey.)

The children are given dietary supplements of Evening Primrose Oil, chosen because it is uniquely a rich source of essential fatty acids and contains both linoleic and gamma-linolenic acid. Some children take it by mouth and others have it rubbed into the skin on the insides of forearms, thighs or abdomen. It is obtained under the name 'Efamol'. In conjunction with this, vitamins are used – vitamin C, B3, B6, and Zinc Sulphate which are obtainable as tablets under the name 'Efavite' (the HACSG also recommends other suppliers). Copies of the *Medical Hypothesis* and accompanying notes for parents which give full instructions for giving the dietary supplements, in correct amounts for all ages, and addresses for the sources of supply, are available from the HACSG for a small fee.

The Group also helps children who have specific food

* See diagram of EFAs on page 201.

allergies or sensitivities, such as milk and dairy products, wheat and so on. A continuous flow of information is available directly from the HACSG and local groups also share ideas and ways in which individual help has been found for their particular children. I have heard the Group criticised for being concerned only with the Feingold diet, but this certainly does not seem to be the case, as you can see. People do, of course, become very excited when they at last find something which actually helps their child. This is very understandable if they have been struggling for years with a problem child and have had little support or advice in the past. They try the food programme suggested and find that it actually works. Who would not be overjoyed at finding relief from a long-term problem which has been ruining their daily life and hindering their child's development? The relief experienced is like walking out of a dark tunnel into the sunshine. No wonder that parents go around with missionary zeal telling the good news to all they meet and in particular telling other parents with children who might benefit likewise. This may give the impression that diet is the only factor.

The HACSG is also interested in behavioural research, and in helping parents obtain an Attendance Allowance, if needed, from the Department of Health; they review books on all aspects of the hyperactive problem and look into the educational needs of hyperactive children. Sally Bunday has also been instrumental in having children returned home who had been taken into care because of their hyperactive-type behaviour problems and organising treatment for them in their own homes. Details regarding hair analysis for estimating mineral deficiencies and toxic metals in children are also supplied by the Group.

The work of the Group is highly professional and very efficient. It deserves all the support it can get in order to continue helping the parents of problem children throughout Britain. Financial support has in the past been sadly lacking and full recognition of the splendid work accomplished is long overdue. There is a desperate need for funds to conduct more research into the subject. What a fertile field this is, with thousands of children to study who have been helped by the HACSG and so many more unaware that aid for the whole family is within reach. How much better is a diagnosis and carefully planned programme at an early age than the need to spend vast sums of money later to sort out complicated behaviour, educational and family problems.

The HACSG has eminent medical and scientific advisers, namely Dr P. J. Barlow, Lecturer in Environmental Health, Dr T. S. G. Davies, MA, BM, BCh, Professor J. W. T. Dickerson, Professor of Nutrition, Dr B. Pickard, Physiologist, Dr Vicky Rippere, BA, MA, PhD, BSc, MPhil, Lecturer in Psychology, Dr A. J. Franklin MRCP, DCH, Consultant Paediatrician, and Professor D. Bryce-Smith, PhD, DSc, CChem, FRIC, Professor of Organic Chemistry.

12   Views of the Medical Profession

The first person to whom parents turn in the event of difficulties with their children is usually their family doctor. Unfortunately the response they receive may not always be very helpful, as you will have seen from the interviews with parents of hyperactive children in the previous part of the book.

I asked a number of doctors if they would mind telling me their views on the subject. The response I received proved poor. Twenty-three doctors did not respond to my enquiry, despite the fact that I enclosed a stamped addressed envelope, made my questionnaire as easy as possible to reply to quickly, and gave space for fuller comments should they wish to give additional views. I realise that doctors are extremely busy people who are constantly bombarded by material via the post, so my enquiry probably represented one more time-consuming inessential best deposited in the waste paper bin. Several doctors returned my enquiry totally blank. Another wrote on the corner of the sheet of paper, 'I am sorry, I cannot' followed by his signature. Another, in answer to my question, 'Would you ever use the term 'hyperactive' to describe the behaviour of some children?' replied, 'No.' All subsequent questions had a dash across the space left for replies and there was no further comment whatsoever.

'I regret I do not feel sufficiently expert in this subject,' appeared in the space for comment on the reply from another doctor.

Dr A. answered my questions in the following way. He does use the term 'hyperactive' to describe the behaviour of some children and bases this on the mother's story and the behaviour of the child in his office. He refers such children to others for help. He considers the possible causes of the condition to be partly mismanagement by parents and partly family difficulties, but does not consider injury at birth plays any part in the possible cause. He does not know if reactions to certain foods or to colouring and additives in foods might have any part in causing the condition, but if parents suggested that the child's problems stemmed from such sources and they needed medication for a health problem he would be willing to prescribe medication without added colouring. He sees the use of drugs to control hyperactivity as necessary only very occasionally and considers that children grow out of the condition. He had not previously heard of the Hyperactive Children's Support Group but would now be willing to recommend suitable families to get in touch with them. There were no further comments he wished to add.

Dr B. likewise uses the term 'hyperactive', but advises parents himself. He sees the possible causes as usually mismanagement by parents or often family difficulties, and very rarely injury at birth. It might be possible that certain foods or colourings and additives cause the condition, but he adds that this is not proven. Very, very occasionally, he feels that it is necessary to prescribe drugs. He says he has no idea if children grow out of the problem or whether it continues into the teens and adulthood. He has heard of the Hyperactive Children's Support Group.

'There is no proof, but there may be something in the idea of using Evening Primrose Oil,' he comments, adding:

There is no proof at all at present that hyperactivity is due to inability to metabolise or manufacture certain fats, nor that allergy is at the root of it, but the idea is interesting and worth pursuing.

However, by far and away the most common cause of hyperactivity is a failure on the part of parents to draw the line beyond which bad behaviour will not be tolerated. The child therefore has to go on being worse and worse be- haved in the hope that the parents will at last become firm and give it some guidelines. Uncontrolled children are miserable and may well be hyperactive. Some parents seem terrified ever to say 'no' or to punish. I get the impression that American parents are even worse than British parents in this respect and of course they are always the ones who have read all about Evening Primrose Oil.

Dr H. says that he is not very conversant with modern theory. Poor sleeping habits, lack of concentration and the inability to sit still, as well as destructiveness and so on, are criteria which cause him to consider the possibility of hyperactivity in a child. He treats the child himself and refers him as necessary. Parental mismanagement, family difficulties, injury at birth, reaction to certain foods or to colouring and additives in foods he sees as all being possible causes of the condition but none convincingly proved. He would provide the child with medicine minus colour if the parents asked for it but he is not convinced regarding the theory. Drugs are not very effective, he feels, but he would prescribe them. He thinks the trend is for hyperactive children to grow out of the problem. He has heard of the Hyperactive Children's Support Group although he does not know how to contact it, but it would seem a sensible thing for him to recommend parents to contact it. He adds that it is 'a very distressing condition for all concerned.'

Dr S. says that she does not use the term 'hyperactive' as a diagnosis:

Definition is precisely the problem. The term usually means that an adult is saying, 'This child is always on the go. I can't keep up. There must be something wrong with him. He must be more active than normal. I will give him a label: hyperactive.' Unless you have a clear criterion for defining normal child activity at different ages, how can you decide that this child's behaviour is outside the normal range? This is a field for clinical psychologists, not one where most doctors have any expertise.

She refers parents to a child guidance centre or the pre-school unit at a hospital in London where clinical psychologists and psychiatric social workers have time to interview them and help them to work out an appropriate strategy.

Dr F. took the trouble to write me a letter enquiring further about my reason for studying the subject and saying that when

I gave more information he would then be prepared to help me. I wrote him a detailed letter but have heard nothing more from him.

A further reply arrived from a doctor who did not want to be quoted, but in general his views were similar to those already expressed. He mentioned that his experience is very limited.

A consultant paediatrician wrote to me as follows:

I first became interested in dietary treatment of children with hyperactivity through my interest in allergic children. Although most medical people are well aware of allergic reactions caused by the inhalation of grass pollen, or horse dander, etc., there is a certain lack of interest and knowledge when it comes to the question of ingested allergens. The detection of food allergens is difficult as skin testing is invariably negative. Hence, one requires the cumbersome use of elimination diets to detect offending allergens.

It was through this period of development that I noticed a number of children whose symptoms of diarrhoea, abdominal pain, etc., ceased, but who showed quite a changed behaviour pattern for the better. Subsequently, I read of the Feingold diet and since then have met a number of children who markedly benefit from either the exclusion of an allergic food substance or whose personality, from using a Feingold diet, shows marked changes for the better.

Naturally, all hyperactive children are not sufferers from food allergy, nor do they all react adversely to salicylate, dyes etc., as hyperactivity is not infrequently found in brain damaged children. It would be nice to have more definite proof, such as *in vitro* tests, to prove the efficacy of such treatment, and until this is done, I doubt if the medical profession in general will accept the fact that ingested foodstuffs can cause alterations in personality.

A doctor referred to as Tony gave his views on the Reading station Radio 210, on the programme 'What's up Doc?' The subject broadcast in February 1983 was 'Hyperactive Children'. The presenter, Graham Ledger, asked him how he reacted to the term 'hyperactive'.

'We get many children brought to the surgery whose parents are having difficulties for one reason or another with a child who seems to be roaring around all over the place, has difficulty sleeping at night – and these are the sort of very broad spectrum of problems that I suppose slot into the definition of hyperactivity,' he replied.

'Do you accept the condition of hyperactivity?' asked Graham Ledger.

'Not as such. As I said before, it is a broad spectrum of problems that I think we are dealing with and hyperactivity, or whatever you like to call it, covers a vast range of problems.

'I think one has to go into that particular situation to find out what is happening. To label them all hyperactive one could overgeneralise and run into problems on that basis.'

The presenter asked the doctor if he felt that allergies associated with food and the environment and lead are factors which play a part in the behaviour of children.

'Maybe. The difficulty with these situations is that a lot of research has not been done. A lot of work has been done and many things have been labelled as being the cause of the particular syndrome but nobody has really done a controlled study on these children, or on adults, come to that, to say that they are basically allergic.'

Graham Ledger mentioned to the doctor that some children have been shown to be allergic to a number of different things and when their diet has been changed, leaving these out, they have returned to normal.

'Yes, you do hear a lot about this – and fine if it works, but on the other hand, is it because one has changed his diet, or is it because the whole situation, the whole family unit, has been treated? These are questions which really have not been answered. Attitudes change, relationships change within the family unit because of the care that people are taking, and certainly the hyperactive child is getting more attention because of this, – and is *that* the reason why he is getting better?'

He was asked about his attitude to local organisations such as 'Helplines' and self-help groups. Did he favour them or feel that they did more harm than good?

'I don't honestly know. My experience of these is very small and I wouldn't like to answer that in any meaningful way.'

Did he think that such groups might give assistance in

coping with the child more than really helping the child himself, or was there an element of both?

'Yes, it comes back to what I said before, more attention, more thought, a change of attitudes. The danger is, of course, that the wrong ideas are perhaps reinforced within these groups, that people tend to get hooked on an idea in the group.'

'Hooked on diet, for example?' asked the presenter. 'They may say, "That's the magic ingredient," whereas they are neglecting to look at what has been happening, that they are becoming aware of the problem themselves?'

'Yes, possibly, that might be the answer,' said the doctor.

Following this interview, Dr Stephen Davies, medical adviser to the Hyperactive Children's Support Group, added some comments on the doctor's personal views. He pointed out that doctors all over Britain, the continent and America are now using the method of diet to deal with this problem and that controlled studies linking behaviour with food allergies have been done. He would supply the references if required. As for the question of diet or the attention being the important factor, he said that when one has treated a number of children in this way it becomes very clear that diet in certain circumstances does have a very dramatic effect and that one is not looking at the effect of the mother's relief because she has something to do. He said that on occasions when the child unwittingly receives something, certain food or a colouring, the behaviour changes again dramatically and that it really has little bearing on what the mother is doing.

'Doctors using this method know that there is really no shadow of a doubt – it is rather like saying, "Does your head hurt when you bang it against a wall?" You only need to do it once or twice, or three times, and you can come to the conclusion that, yes, it probably does. With respect, it becomes very evident, quickly, that diet can and does influence behaviour.'

(Interview reproduced by permission of Radio 210 and the doctor concerned).

Dr James Dobson, Associate Clinical Professor of Paediatrics, USC School of Medicine, gives some interesting views on the subject in *The Strong-Willed Child*, a book which helps parents to cope in a logical way with the problems their children present.

Here are some of his remarks on hyperactivity:

> Hyperactivity often appears related to damage to the central nervous system, although it can also be caused by emotional stress and fatigue. Some authorities believe that virtually all children born through the birth canal (that is, not by caesarean section) are likely to sustain damage to brain tissue during the birth process. The difference between patients who are severely affected (and are called cerebral palsied) and those who have no obvious symptoms, may reflect three variables:
> (1) Where the damage is located; (2) How massive the lesion is; and (3) How quickly it occurred. Thus, it is possible that some hyperactive children were afflicted by an unidentified brain interference very early which caused no other symptoms or problems. I must emphasise, however, that this explanation is merely speculative and that the medical understanding of this disorder is far from complete. (p. 147)

He goes on to ask how parents can tell the difference between normal activity and genuine hyperactivity and how they can decide whether a child's problem is the result of emotional or physical impairment.

> These questions are difficult to answer, and few parents have the training to resolve them. Your best resource in evaluating your child's problem is your paediatrician or family physician. Even he may have to guess at a diagnosis and its cause. He can, however, make a complete medical evaluation and then refer you, if necessary, to other professionals for specific assistance. Your child may require the services of a remedial reading teacher or a speech and hearing therapist or a psychologist who can assess intellectual and perceptual abilities and offer management advice. You should not try to cope with an excessively active child if this additional support and consultation is available. (p. 150).

What is the role of nutrition? he asks:

The role of nutrition in hyperactivity is a very controversial issue which I am not qualified to resolve; I can only offer my opinion on the subject. The American people have been told that hyperactivity is a product of red food colouring, too much sugar intake, inadequate vitamins, and many related causes resulting from poor nutrition. I don't doubt for a moment that improper eating habits have the capacity to destroy us physically and could easily be related to the phenomenon of hyperactivity. However, I am of the opinion that the writers of many faddish books on this subject are trying to make their guesses sound like proven facts. Many of the answers are not yet available, which explains why so many 'authorities' disagree violently among themselves.

The nutritionists whom I respect most highly are those who take a cautious, scientific approach to these complex questions. I am suspicious of the self-appointed experts who bypass their own professional publications and come directly to the lay public with unsupported conclusions which even their colleagues reject.

The above paragraph may irritate some parents who are following the advice of a lone-wolf nutritional writer. To those readers I can only say, 'Do what succeeds.' If your child is more calm and sedate when avoiding certain foods, then use your judgement as you continue the successful dietary regimen. Your opinion is probably as valid as mine. (p. 151).

Then he comes to the problem of disciplining a hyperactive child:

It is often assumed that an excessively active child should be indulged because he has a physical problem. I couldn't disagree more. Every youngster needs the security of defined limits, and the hyperactive boy or girl is no exception. Such a child should be held responsible for his behaviour, like the rest of the family. Of course, your level of expectation must be adjusted to fit his limitations. For example, most children can be required to sit in a chair for disciplinary reasons, whereas the hyperactive child would not be able to remain there. Similarly, spankings are sometimes ineffective with a highly excitable little bundle of electricity. As with every aspect of parenthood, disciplinary measures for the hyperactive child must be suited to his unique characteristics and needs. (p. 156)

(Abstract from the book, *The Strong-Willed Child*, Tyndale House Publishers, by James C. Dobson, PhD Associate Clinical Professor of Paediatrics, USC School of Medicine. Used by permission.)

Dr Stephen Davies, MA, BM, BCh, medical adviser to the Hyperactive Children's Support Group, gave his views on the subject of hyperactivity in a lecture entitled 'The integrated approach to the management and prevention of hyperactivity' at a conference in 1982 organised by the Support Group. Copies of his 'live' conference recording (and that of other speakers at the conference) are available from INTER-FORUM (see addresses).

He began his lecture by noting the following:

Many GPs fail to recognise that there is a genuine problem child in front of them and tend to fob the mother off as a neurotic or incompetent or inadequate mother, unable to cope with a boisterous child. Others offer the mother tranquillizers and some even give the child drugs to make him or her calm down or sleep. Child psychiatric clinics often offer little more.

He says that we need to look at the environment which we have created in order to understand why hyperactivity is occurring.

We have burdened it with many noxious substances, poisons, chemicals, heavy metals and so on that just weren't around to the same degree, if at all, in former ages. We also rely on foods that are stripped of much of the nutritional value and to which have been added all these various chemicals, insecticides, pesticides, preservatives, antioxidents, emulsifiers, colouring, and so on. On purely theoretical grounds, if one were to conduct an experiment, to change an environment so dramatically you would be looking for the ways in which this changed environment would have an impact on the biochemistry and function of the group of animals or a species. In this context, I would like to look at the factors which influence behaviour and apply it to the hyperactive child. Perhaps in this way we can formulate a rational approach to the treatment of hyperactive as well as mental disorders, since the best treatment of any condition should invariably be based, where possible, on an understanding of the underlying factors involved. The trouble with drug therapy is that it is based on very little understanding of what is going on. It is usually just a purely symptomatic treatment and doesn't really address the problem in hand at all.

Dr Davies notes that nutrient intake has a direct impact on the biochemistry of the body, as do toxic elements and compounds which are injected, swallowed, inhaled and applied in many different ways. Nutrients also alter the way in which toxins affect the biochemistry, as does structure – for example, the lack of a vital organ makes the biochemistry of the body change rapidly. Maladaptive food and chemical reactions (basically 'allergies' in the broadest sense of the word) also have an affect on the body's biochemistry. Another factor is the person himself, his personality, what he is.

'In looking at the underlying mechanism of disease, if we do not look at these factors, we are going to be looking at something other than the causes of the problem. I think it is a fundamental inadequacy of much of modern medicine and much of the research which is going on,' he said.

Much research over the last ten years has shown that toxic metals, even at relatively low levels, do actually influence mental function. Lead is found present in human beings at levels up to 1000 times greater than man originally had to cope with in his body, he notes.

'We should expect to see failure to adapt to that increase.'

As well as toxic metals there are all the additives in our food, and petro-chemical derivatives and things in daily use that were not present in any quantity in our past. It is accepted that drugs affect mental function.

'Doctors rely on these toxins to produce a desirable effect –

but I think that as time goes by we will learn more and more of the harmful effects of these substances.'

People tend to think that there is no malnutrition in this country. An increasing number of studies show that it is quite rife. Many people live on refined carbohydrates which have been stripped of the essential nutrients. These include white sugar, white flour and any foods containing these.

'The influence of excess refined carbohydrates on mental function can really be quite profound.' Hypoglycemia (low blood glucose) can be caused by an excess amount of refined carbohydrates, too.

'There is a lot of evidence to show that many hyperactive children as well as many mentally disturbed individuals have a disrupted, abnormal glucose metabolism. This is brought about by a number of things: excess stress, too many refined carbohydrates and concomitant deficiencies.'

He discussed the need for vitamins and the fact that allergies tend to run in families but are not necessarily genetic. Many of the hyperactive children also have eczema, hay fever and asthma.

Dr Davies has a very positive view on the management of children who are hyperactive. We cannot do a great deal to alter certain factors, for example, we cannot remove lead from petrol immediately. However, parents can put their child on the Feingold food programme. If they then take the child to their own doctor he is likely to be unsympathetic. The reason for this is that many doctors have not been introduced to the concept of the underlying mechanics of disease – the importance of nutrition, the influence upon mental function and the biochemistry as a whole that toxins can have.

'Doctors not taking this approach are actually depriving themselves of much professional satisfaction,' he thinks.

He sees the integrated approach to hyperactive children as very important. This includes a physical examination and investigation with a full dietary history and nutritional assessment. Any vitamin deficiencies are important, as is the presence of toxic metal in the body and correction of mineral levels. In addition he feels that it is very important to know the social history and any problems within the family such as allergy, severe mental disturbance, schizophrenia, and so on.

He has been very surprised at times at the power of the dietary therapy, even in circumstances when there are the most awful social conditions which cannot be altered. Behavioural treatment should not be neglected. Tender loving care and positive reinforcement are very important. The child should be told with as much force that he is doing right as parents use to tell him he is doing wrong! Dr Davies also thinks that once the child has responded to this overall treatment, it is important for him to get adequate rest and fresh air, even if he previously slept little and went to bed late. Parents often notice an added improvement if this is taken into consideration.

Dr Davies adds some warnings about the mother's over-concern about the environment when using dietary therapy.

'It is terribly important not to make the child himself junior to the diet,' he says. The child needs to realise that he is behaving better; it is not his additive-free food that behaves better, but himself. The additive-free food and no refined carbohydrates, and so on, help him to be a good boy.

The concept of biochemical individuality should be borne in mind, stresses Dr Davies, in order to understand why one person is affected by certain things and another is not affected. One child may not respond to the Feingold diet programme, but may show an improvement after detoxification from lead. If not, he may improve on a low refined carbohydrate diet or when the nutrient deficiencies are corrected. It may require several different ways or many ways in order to produce the therapeutic response:

> Done sensibly, these treatments are simple, they are harmless, as far as we know, and can have a great impact, not only on the child's enjoyment of life and ease of growing up, but also on the family harmony – not to mention mum's tattered nerves! This is obviously a much healthier approach than just drugging, or ignoring.

The moral responsibility to bring about change lies on the shoulders of each of us who has an understanding of the mechanism involved. The trend of creating a yet unsafer environment for our children and our children's children still continues. We insist on adding lead to our petrol, thereby contaminating our precious atmosphere. As a nation we continue to eat more refined carbohydrates each year; we continue to strip our soil yet further of vital nutrients; we continue to pump more drugs and chemicals into our systems; we continue to consume yet more quantities of artificial food additives whose safety has not yet been proven.

Dr Damien Downing MBBS, LicAc, has an Alternative Medical Practice. To round off this chapter, he has contributed a discussion of his views on hyperactivity and its causes.

It is said that people learn best by experience, and doctors are no exception to this. Having had my surgery nearly demolished on several occasions by small patients has undoubtedly assisted me towards a belief in the existence of hyperactivity. Having a son who suffers a minor degree of the same problem has furthermore helped me to sympathise greatly with parents of such children.

It is clear that one of the most important things that can be done for such a family unit in the consultation is to reassure them that they are not imagining the problem, nor is it their fault. Most of these children have at least started on the merry-go-round of remedial teachers, psychologists and psychiatrists, welfare workers and the like. Each professional tends to provide his own explanation of the problem, based no doubt, as is my own, on his own past experiences and prejudices. Parents are frequently told that the child's disturbance is the result of abnormally early potty training, or the lack of potty training, the lack of affection, or a surfeit of affection. Very often all of these are stated about the same child by different people at different times.

It is little wonder, therefore, that by the umpteenth visit to a doctor or other health worker the parents of a hyperactive child are frequently highly anxious and frustrated, and this frustration may well manifest itself as aggression. It is all too easy for a doctor to assume that this high level of parental emotion is the cause, rather than the effect of the child's abnormal behaviour. Indeed the longer the child's problem remains unresolved the more likely it is that these frustrations will put a strain on the parent-child relationship, and thus a vicious spiral of deteriorating behaviour on both sides can be entered.

There are two factors which appear to help this problem directly: firstly, I have never met a parent who did not benefit from the support and advice given to them by groups such as the Hyperactive Children's Support Group. Even if the only effect of joining such a group is to reassure the mother and father that they are not alone in their problem, this can benefit them enormously, and enable them to get their feet on the ground and view matters with a greater degree of perspective.

Secondly, it is part of the mythology of our society that doctors are almost infallible, and patients and their relatives therefore tend to believe what they say without question. Attempting to believe several conflicting statements simultaneously is, however, a step on the road to insanity, and it is therefore important for parents to approach their doctors with the healthy, consumerist cynicism that they would apply to a washing machine or a new car. Even if this means that they may only hear those things which they want to be told, it still enables them to acquire a greater degree of control over their own destiny and that of their children, which is essential if they are going to deal with the problem rather than simply live with it. After all, the doctor's surgery is only demolished for a few minutes, while the family home has to bear the strain day in and day out. Parents must have the final decision on what they can or cannot, will or will not do to help the child with hyperactivity.

What is hyperactivity?

The word 'hyperactive' is a very large peg, on which a considerable variety of different disturbances of behaviour have been hung. The problem is not so much that it is so wide a term as to be meaningless, as that it is simply an extremely broad and meaningful one. Clearly it will soon be necessary to subdivide and rename the different types of problem within this term. It would be possible to do this by means of the different types of behavioural disturbances displayed, by the associated physical and psychological symptoms found, by the degree of severity of the problem, or by the causative factors of the disorder.

Elsewhere in this book there are several descriptions of the type of symptoms that occur in hyperactivity and a long list of such symptoms is not likely to clarify matters greatly. Several things do appear to be true about hyperactivity, however. The first has not been scientifically demonstrated and would indeed be difficult to so demonstrate. It is nevertheless a strong impression of mine and other people and fits well with the available scientific theories. This is the theory that the susceptibility to being triggered into hyperactive behaviour is not something that a child simply either has or does not have, but something that occurs in a continuous gradation of shades of severity, from the nonexistent to the extreme. It is likely that such a variable severity will in fact turn out to display what is called a 'normal' distribution. That is to say, statistical analysis of a population would probably find that there was a particular curve for this susceptibility. By definition, most individuals will be average and the more extreme degrees either of susceptibility or non-susceptibility will occur less and less frequently. The same curve can be shown to occur for intelligence, for physical ability, for height or weight and so on. The major implication of this is that it makes it meaningless to say 'there are X thousand hyperactive children in this country'; all children will have a greater or lesser degree of susceptibility to the problem and those factors which influence some children dramatically will have a slight influence on many more. In other words, the problem is not one that is unique to a small section of the population but is shared by us all.

A recent study showed that hyperactivity, allergic rhinitis and enuresis occurred more commonly together than would be expected. It is also commonplace that many children with hyperactivity also suffer from eczema. These two facts demonstrate the importance of allergies in hyperactivity but, as mentioned below, there are other factors which must be taken into account. It is certainly true that very often hyperactivity is only one, albeit the most distressing, of a number of symptoms of a generalised illness.

There are a number of factors which appear to have a bearing on the development of hyperactivity and at this stage in our knowledge it is not clear whether they interact together or whether they can operate completely independently. The three major factors are:

1 *Allergies* Many hyperactive children have allergies to foods, chemicals, and/or inhalants which can be demonstrated by various means of testing and the treatment of which will cure or substantially benefit the hyperactivity.

2 *Salicylates* A large percentage of hyperactive children appear to suffer from a metabolic problem which is made worse by taking in salicylates, which occur in food colourings and a number of foods and also by lack of certain essential nutrients.

3 *Toxic metals* Whether by the same mechanism as in 2, or by an independent one, it certainly appears that many hyperactive children are affected by high levels of lead, cadmium and other toxic metals.

The salicylate hypothesis
Essential fatty acids are of course vital to health. They are naturally occurring fats, which are chains of carbon atoms with an 'acid' radical at one end. The feature which gives them importance is the presence of double bonds between pairs of carbon atoms, which can be opened up to provide sites for new chemical structures to be built. In the body they are metabolised to prostaglandins, to steroid hormones and to lipids, which are components of all cell walls. They may turn out to be the factor in plant fats as opposed to animal fats which protect us against coronary thrombosis, against cancer, and possibly even against schizophrenia. They are deficient in many modern diets as a consequence of the high intake of animal fats and of mechanical and chemical processes used to produce vegetable oils. Since the double bond is what makes it possible for fats to go rancid, it is clearly in the interests of food producers to avoid unsaturated fats, because of their shorter shelf life.

The theory developed by David Horrobin and other North American workers regarding hyperactivity, is that hyperactive children have a deficiency, or a vulnerability to external factors, of a particular enzyme system involved in producing prostaglandins from essential fatty acids. The particular prostaglandin which this system produces, prostaglandin El, appears to have an important role in controlling levels of behavioural excitation, in controlling the functioning of the immune system and in adjusting the fluid balance and fluid input/output by means of the kidneys and the thirst mechanism. The enzyme is, like so many others in the body, dependent on the presence of several co-enzyme factors, including zinc, magnesium, vitamins B3 and B6 and vitamin C. It is vulnerable to the effects of a number of chemicals, including salicylates, alcohol, medical drugs and such factors as stress, raised temperature and exertion. Naturally, it is also affected by shortages of the essential fatty acid which it metabolises. This system is therefore susceptible to a number of factors and it may be necessary to deal with all of them in order to get it working satisfactorily.

On the assumption that the major factor damaging this enzyme was the intake of salicylates, Dr Ben Feingold in the United States treated a number of children successfully with a diet which eliminated all salicylates, both synthetic and naturally occurring. The alternative approach is to supplement the enzyme system with large quantities of the essential fatty acid and of various co-factors necessary for the reaction to occur. A provisional regime has been worked out and details of it are available from the Hyperactive Children's Support Group. This is theoretically sound as far as it goes, but the major problem is that it is almost impossible to take into account all of the factors involved in such an enzyme system without doing careful clinical and laboratory work on each individual patient. In practice, my impression is that around 30% of hyperactive children will respond dramatically to the proposed regime, which involves giving Evening Primrose Oil (a rich source of gamma-linolenic acid, an essential fatty acid), together with zinc and pyridoxine. Unfortunately, there seems to be no way of telling in advance which children will respond. It is therefore worth a try for most sufferers, but parents should not be too disheartened if the results are disappointing. There are many other factors involved, most of which are accessible to treatment of one form or another. Indeed, it could well be that this will turn out to be the central factor in hyperactivity and that allergies, toxic metals and all the other

CIS-LINOLEIC ACID (obtainable only from food intake)

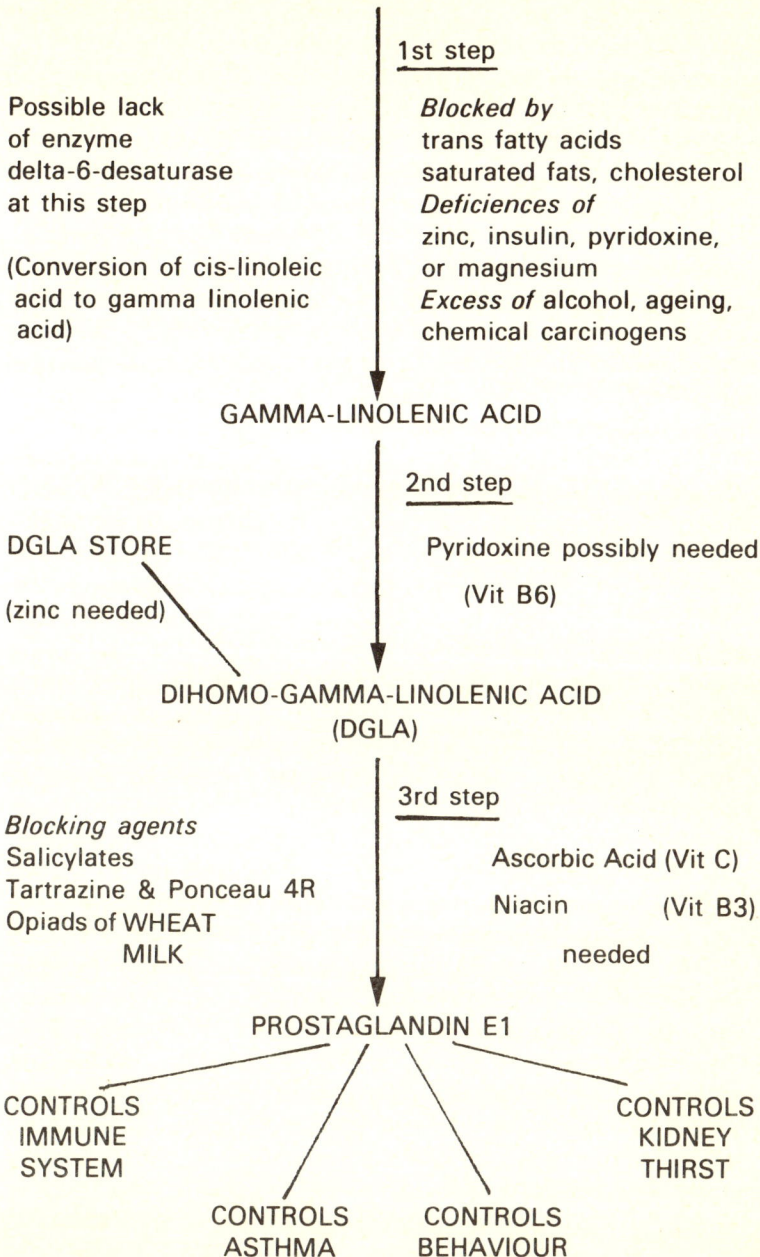

1st step

Possible lack
of enzyme
delta-6-desaturase
at this step

(Conversion of cis-linoleic
acid to gamma linolenic
acid)

Blocked by
trans fatty acids
saturated fats, cholesterol
Deficiences of
zinc, insulin, pyridoxine,
or magnesium
Excess of alcohol, ageing,
chemical carcinogens

GAMMA-LINOLENIC ACID

2nd step

DGLA STORE

(zinc needed)

Pyridoxine possibly needed

(Vit B6)

DIHOMO-GAMMA-LINOLENIC ACID
(DGLA)

3rd step

Blocking agents
Salicylates
Tartrazine & Ponceau 4R
Opiads of WHEAT
MILK

Ascorbic Acid (Vit C)

Niacin   (Vit B3)

needed

PROSTAGLANDIN E1

CONTROLS
IMMUNE
SYSTEM

CONTROLS
KIDNEY
THIRST

CONTROLS
ASTHMA

CONTROLS
BEHAVIOUR

factors are actually operating through this mechanism. Only time will tell.

1 Allergies

The debate over food allergies looks likely to continue for some time. Do they exist? How common are they? Are they involved only in classical allergic problems such as asthma and eczema, or do they also cause psychological disturbances, rheumatoid arthritis, migraines and many other diseases? In part, this is a result of disagreement over the use of the word 'allergy'. Many conventional immunologists consider that it should only be used to refer to the atopic disorders (asthma, eczema and rhinitis), while the American Clinical Ecology movement and a number of doctors in this country, as well as patient support groups and other lay people, use the term to refer to any unpleasant or symptom-producing reactions to foods. It is certainly true that there are a number of different mechanisms whereby food can produce adverse reactions and the salicylate hypothesis is a good example of this. There are many others, including the reaction to tyramine-containing foods which produces migraines in some people, the susceptibility to histamine which can cause reactions to shellfish and egg, and certain inbuilt mechanisms which make people unable to digest or metabolise particular foods. My inclination, in common with a number of other doctors, is to allow the use of the word 'allergy' to refer to any reaction which produces symptoms. In the context of hyperactivity, experience has shown that many children improve when certain incriminated foods are eliminated from their diet and these children may not necessarily respond to essential fatty acid supplements.

There is no theoretical debate over the fact that eczema and rhinitis are most commonly due to allergies, and in practice there is good evidence that bed wetting may be produced by allergic problems also. Since hyperactivity appears to fall into a symptom complex with these diseases, this makes it more likely that hyperactivity itself is an allergic phenomenon. The problem is complicated by the fact that, while many azo dyes (food colourings) are structurally related to the salicylate molecule and may produce symptoms for that reason, it is also possible for people to develop genuine antibody-mediated allergic reactions to tartrazine and other colourings. However, it is possible for children and adults to react to many other foods and chemicals, which have nothing to do with salicylates. Also, it may well be, as mentioned earlier, that there is a universal stimulant effect from such chemicals, which affects everybody to a greater or lesser degree and that the children who have been classed as hyperactive are simply more susceptible than others – or even simply taking in higher doses than others.

If parents wish to help their children by finding out whether they have allergies, it is necessary for them to have some understanding of the problem and they should probably read one of the excellent books available on the subject. The problem is too complex to explain in detail here, but a few facts are worth stating. Only a small minority of allergies to foods, or even to inhalants, appear to be of the 'fixed' type, such as the acute hives produced by occasional exposure to shellfish. The large majority of allergies are slow to develop and may be 'masked'. This means that a certain normal dosage comes to be treated by the body as its normal intake and does not produce acute symptoms. It is only when the intake is greatly reduced and withdrawal symptoms develop, or greatly increased to produce overdosage, that the patient is at all aware of the possibility that he or she might be reacting to foods.

For this reason, and also because there is very often an addictive component to these food reactions, such problems tend to arise with foods which are eaten regularly, possibly several times a day. When the foods are cut out of the diet, there may be a withdrawal period of a few days, during which the child gets worse before getting better. It is very easy, during this period, to assume that the alteration in the diet is making the patient worse and it is therefore better for him to return to the original diet. If one persists for a few days longer, however, one may find a remarkable improvement occurs.

Although it is possible to work through all of the likely foods systematically without any outside help, it is certainly far from easy. The first step should be to obtain a good book such as *Uncovering Hidden Food Allergies* (Crook and Crook) and to read it carefully and plan the campaign. If you feel that this is too difficult a task, then professional advice will be needed, ideally from a sympathetic doctor. While it is true that there are bigots in the medical profession as in any other, I fear that general practitioners are often unjustly condemned by people who assume that they will not be responsive to such ideas as these. If you are truly unable to find medical help, it is one of the roles of support groups to help you out of this position.

In deciding which foods to investigate first, bear in mind several points. Firstly, it is unlikely that your child will react to foods which he has very infrequently, at least not without your noticing it at the time. Secondly, it may well be difficult at first to change his diet because children, like adults, tend to have paradoxical attitudes to the foods to which they are allergic – they either like them or loathe them. The foods to which they do not react they are either indifferent to, or simply reject because they prefer the allergic ones. This means that you may experience a certain amount of 'consumer resistance' at first, but as the allergies are sorted out, the child's individual tastes will genuinely alter. Thirdly, the commonest foods to which children have allergies are milk, egg, and food colourings. However, this is a statistical statement and it may well be that your child will react to beef and wheat (both in hamburgers) and beans (provided in the tinned, baked variety).

If, as is not uncommon, there are reactions to at least five different foods, then cutting out only one of them is unlikely to produce much more than a 20% improvement, which may be difficult to spot. For these reasons, a systematic approach is essential. From a practical point of view, the redeeming factor of elimination dieting is that it does not matter in the least how a reaction to a food is produced, if avoiding it makes the victim better. Finally, it must be borne in mind that drugs taken for the problem, and this includes skin creams for eczema, may blunt or otherwise alter a person's reaction to elimination dieting. This can usually be overcome by simply carrying on the process rather longer.

2 Nutrition

Recent work has suggested that the average British diet may be unhealthy, in that it is inadequate in certain vitamins and other nutrients. This is of course disputed by the food industry. As well as a possible abnormally high requirement for essential fatty acids, hyperactive children are going to need vitamins and essential minerals just as much as any other child, and possibly more, because they are unwell. Stress, exertion and any form of ill health invariably increase requirements for essential nutrients and minerals. It is therefore necessary to ensure that a sufferer from hyperactivity receives a good healthy diet, rich in whole grains, fresh fruit and vegetables. It may well be necessary also to provide them with supplements of particular vitamins or minerals, but this is a complicated business and parents are unlikely to succeed without specialist advice. Again, the ideal first port of call is probably a support group, which will include a number of parents who have worked through the same problem themselves.

While it is not possible to associate hyperactivity clearly with any single vitamin deficiency, such deficiencies in general may produce children who are easily tired, listless and miserable, irritable, have poor resistance to infection and do less well at school, both in class and sports. Since an adequate supply of essential nutrients is needed for any self healing, it may also be needed to enable children to recover from hyperactivity and its associate problems.

3   Toxic metals

Toxic minerals such as lead, cadmium and aluminium, were once thought to cause medical problems very rarely. It is now apparent that they are an increasing problem, particularly in urban environments. There is a growing body of evidence to associate them with hyperactivity, dyslexia, behavioural disturbances in general and various other forms of ill health.

Lead is of course still emitted in petrol fumes and since it forms large particles it tends to sink down towards the ground and the most vulnerable members of the public to this exposure are children in push chairs. The developing nervous systems of children are also more vulnerable to such exposures. Lead is also present in tobacco fumes and in a number of old paints used in houses, as well as in old lead pipes. Any or all of these factors may be involved in raising a child's lead burden. Cadmium is present in tobacco smoke as well and these two minerals may be the reason why the children of heavy smokers are three times more likely than the children of non smokers to be dyslexic. Cadmium is also emitted from smelters and from various other industrial processes, as are aluminium and arsenic. Although very high levels of these metals are rare and it is easy to deny the existence of the problem, slow chronic exposures over months and years can build up a toxic burden in a child's body that it may be unable to handle. Moreover, most of these minerals interact to produce complementary damaging effects on the nervous system.

Many researchers now think that there is no such thing as a safe level of lead, in the same way as there is no such thing as a universally safe level of radiation, because both may produce problems in susceptible individuals at a level so low as to produce no effect in the majority of cases. Such elements are also antagonistic to essential minerals such as zinc, which can indeed be used to encourage the body to excrete toxic minerals. If a child is deficient in zinc, therefore, he is likely to be more vulnerable to a raised lead level.

There are three ways of testing for the presence of such minerals. Measurement of the blood level of lead or other minerals is unreliable because it may vary rapidly throughout the day and because it may not reflect the level of lead stored in bones and hair and elsewhere. There are certain other biochemical tests, such as the delta amino laevulenic acid test on urine for lead, which show when generalised damage to the body is occurring; this is a useful monitor for high levels in adults but does not take account of the increased vulnerability of children's nervous systems. The ideal method is probably hair mineral analysis, which can now be performed by a number of professional laboratories, but which may again need interpretation by a trained doctor or other health worker.

Bio-energetic medicine

There are three main 'bio-energetic' systems which may be employed to help hyperactivity sufferers. Acupuncture is not often practised on children under the age of 7, but the less distressing form, acupressure, can be used. There is some evidence to show that it can help a wide range of metabolic and other disorders and many children take surprisingly well to it. It is essential that it should be practised by a skilled practitioner and recourse to one of the professional bodies may be necessary in order to find such a person. Homœopathy has been shown to be successful in some cases of hyperactivity and it can certainly do several things. The use of homœopathic preparations of lead appear to encourage the excretion of toxic lead burdens from the body; homœopathic coffee, which would be a stimulant in normal doses, in the minute doses used by homœopaths acts to block other stimulant effects; it may also be possible to use homœopathy to block reactions to a number of other chemicals and foods to which children are allergic. My children find a homœopathic preparation of chlorine, taken 30 minutes before swimming, prevents the red eyes produced by swimming pool chlorine. It may also help to protect those children who react with more generalised symptoms to chlorine. Osteopathy and in particular the cranial and occipito-sacral techniques, has been successful in calming a number of hyperactive children, albeit temporarily, and does often appear to improve the behaviour and sociability of more severely brain damaged children.

The great advantage of these forms of treatment is that it is very difficult to do any harm with them. The disadvantage appears to be that they work quite well if the body has the ability to heal itself, because they operate essentially by activating the body's self healing mechanisms in some manner; however, if there is a major food allergy, nutrient deficiency, toxic metal burden or other biochemical problem, it is unlikely that bio-energetic treatments will produce more than a short-lived and partial improvement. In my experience, they very often enable patients to get half way better and then the progress appears to be blocked. If the biochemical problems are then sorted out, the improvement can be dramatic and certainly this will make bio-energetic treatments much more effective. Acupressure and osteopathy, in common with hydrotherapy, massage and various other physical therapies, have the advantage that touch has a soothing effect on many hyperactive children, just as it can have on all of us.

The future
Many parents of hyperactive children have been told by doctors at one time or another that they should not worry as their child will grow out of it. It would be nice to think this is

true, but there is no good evidence to support it. Unfortunately it is very difficult to predict quite what will happen to these unfortunate children. Since most of the ones who have been identified by the HACSG have therefore been treated and got better, they are no use as a group to study for observing the long term effect of the disorder. Also, the existence of the disease has only recently been recognised, whether because of increasing knowledge or increase in the problem, is not clear, so follow-through into adult life has hardly been possible. No clear indication of the long term prognosis can therefore be given.

Nevertheless, two things can certainly be said. An improvement in the diet of children will inevitably improve their long term health prospects, in every aspect from dental caries to bowel cancer. In the same way, if their behaviour is benefited, their school learning will improve and they will have a far greater chance of growing into normal, healthy adults. Moreover, it is certainly clear that in behavioural disorder as in many other disorders, chronic ill health is made up of repeated small bouts of acute ill health. The more you protect your child against health problems in the short term, therefore, the less the cumulative damage to his or her system in the long term.

13   Help from the Psychologists

THE EDUCATIONAL PSYCHOLOGIST
Hyperactive children often experience learning difficulties in
addition to various problems of behaviour, mood swings, and
overactivity. Children described as hypoactive, too, often
share similar problems with regard to education. Difficulty
with learning to read and spell, or to understand maths, often
arises. In the classroom hyperactive children tend to disrupt
attempts to provide a quiet working atmosphere for themselves
and their fellow pupils and are restless and inattentive. Such
children are usually referred to an educational psychologist
some time during their educational career. The school may call
for such assistance to aid them in dealing with the problems
presented and to find ways of helping the child in his learning.
The parents may go directly to see an educational psychologist
themselves if they are concerned about the child's behaviour in
school and his progress, or lack of it. A surprisingly large
number of people do not know what services exist to help their
child and if they have heard of educational psychologists have a
totally wrong conception of the role they play.

Recently I met two educational psychologists, one from
Berkshire and the other from an adjoining county. They do not
look at a child and at once label him 'hyperactive', but look at
various aspects and consider his needs. One of the psychologists
told me that children with this kind of problem need far less
stimulation in the classroom. They usually work better in a
corner of a room which has nothing near them to distract
them. The ideal place would appear to be a room with windows
set high, too high for the child to be distracted by events
outside, and with little on the walls to divert his attention from
his work. Lacking this, an area screened from the activities of

the other children, to form a cubicle, often aids their concentration and attention to detail. Tape recorders are a good way to confine attention to the matter in hand, with the child listening through head phones. If as much unnecessary stimulation is removed as possible such children will be aided in their learning.

Prior to entering school, it is often better for the child to attend a nursery school rather than a play group, as they find it difficult to fit into the less structured play group situation. They need structure and boundaries, although they appear to want complete freedom. Some hyperactive children settle well into nursery groups which are run at ESN schools (Educationally Subnormal) and transfer to a normal school at five years of age.

In the case of the child just beginning school at five years old the initial problem is to teach him how to learn. It may be that the child will benefit by having a welfare assistant to help him settle into school, gradually withdrawing her aid at a later stage. This may be preferable, in that the child attends a normal school, but the additional assistant helps him to integrate and to learn to work and relieves the teacher of the extra burden. Some children, however, find even this too much to cope with initially, or it may be thought preferable for them to attend an assessment unit with fewer children and more adult help and a quieter situation. If by seven years of age the child is still in need of special help there are junior units which can help (often part-time) until the age of 11. Here again there is more adult help, and a smaller group than is possible in a normal classroom. Pupils are taught to sit down and work in a quiet atmosphere. Special teaching materials are used to aid learning. The child is encouraged to work as part of a group.

The 1981 Education Act states that the individual needs of the child must be met; if economical this will be within the local authority, but if not, outside the area. For example, my foster son experienced educational difficulties and spent some time at an adolescent assessment unit. There appeared to be no suitable school to meet his needs in our home area, so he now boards at a school some 200 miles away. The Warnock Report recommended that children should be catered for within normal schools, not by segregating children according to their physical, mental or educational handicaps, but providing for their needs where they are. This is beginning to be implemented. This means that the needs of children who have problems related to hyperactivity should be catered for within the system, and will not be dealt with as a separate group, but that help should be available to provide for their special needs.

Many parents of hyperactive children have had a bad experience in finding help for their children. Some parents feel that they are not receiving any help for the child and are prepared to pay for a private assessment of their child's ability. I asked the educational psychologist if this seemed a good thing to do.

'No,' he said. 'The parents may have the child assessed elsewhere, but if the psychologist lives outside the area where the child resides he will be unable to recommend a suitable school near the child's home or arrange the best help for him. The parents may find themselves with an assessment which is of little use without the follow up.'

In order to find help and have the child's ability assessed, the Local Education Officer (at the Education Department) should be contacted. He will inform the parents of where they can see an educational psychologist. They do not need to see a doctor first in order to be referred to the service. Individual psychologists are almost all trained and prepared to work with hyperactive children. They will, if necessary, visit the child's home and guide the parents in the day-to-day management of the child, including the use of sleep programmes tailormade to suit individual children and their parents. 'Time out' as a way of modifying the behaviour of the child is often recommended with the child being removed from the situation of conflict to another room for a few minutes at a time. It is very important, pointed out the psychologist, that the child should not be sent to his own room, the toilet, or his playroom, but to a place other than those he uses for specific purposes.

I asked one of the educational psychologists if he recommends parents to contact the Hyperactive Children's Support Group. He had not heard of it and showed caution in recommending parents to such a group as he felt that it might make them feel that the child has been labelled and that there is nothing further that can be done to help the child. I told him of

212 PROFESSIONAL VIEWS ON HYPERACTIVITY

some of the things that the Support Group recommend, including the Feingold Food Programme. He felt that if the Group offered something positive and that if it recommended a diet based on research, he would feel that it could be a great help to the children.

The other educational psychologist I met at a meeting organised by a group of parents who have hyperactive or allergic children and most are members of the Hyperactive Children's Support Group. She is therefore fully aware of the Group's activities and the support they offer to parents. She sees the value of removing from the child's diet anything which may be causing his behaviour to be difficult or slowing his ability to learn. She also sees the need to help the children and their parents, as not all the difficulties are removed immediately by changes in diet. The children have often built up patterns of behaviour over the years with which parents need help to cope, and their education may be behind children of their own age. The work of the Support Group and the educational psychologist can therefore, she feels, go hand in hand in providing help for the child and support for the parents.

THE CLINICAL PSYCHOLOGIST

As I look back over my daughter's childhood, I realise that we tried to alter her behaviour so that life in our household could run smoothly. We were not familiar with the approach used by psychologists and were not attempting to use a particular method to help her. We just looked at the problems she presented and tried to overcome them one or two at a time. Having written Tanya's story I felt that it would be very interesting to see how a clinical psychologist views the subject and how he would deal with the associated problems. What advice could other parents with hyperactive or very difficult children receive that I had not found?

Dr Martin Herbert is Professor of Clinical Psychology at the Department of Psychology, Leicester University. He agreed to discuss with me his views on dealing with the problem caused by hyperactivity. I found him to be very interested and involved with the behaviour of children, not someone who has theories neatly worked out, but is far removed from the subject of his study. He lectures to students, it is true, but he is also closely involved with problem children and aids their parents. Both he and his students work with children as he takes them through their studies.

First of all, I wondered how Dr Herbert defined hyperactivity. Did he consider that a child who slept well at night but became overactive in the daytime could be termed hyperactive?

'A hyperactive child is not necessarily overactive by day and night,' he replied. 'There may be variations in his activity depending on the time of day, the person he is with or the circumstances in which he finds himself: not only is he extremely active, but there is a fragmented quality to his behaviour which is goalless. Some claim the problem is part of a more general conduct disorder which is combined with overactivity. The child is coercive in various ways, has tantrums and is not always aware of the views of other people; as such he is egocentric.'

Dr Herbert thinks it essential to study the child carefully to see when and where the behaviour problems occur and in what situations he is better or worse. He assesses whether the child is difficult and hyperactive with certain people, in certain places, or at certain times. He carries out a detailed evaluation of the child's behaviour before he decides that the child is hyperactive. Sometimes the description is used to excuse certain behaviour problems, he feels, and rather than trying to cope with the problem in the optimistic hope, indeed expectation, that the child can change, the label 'hyperactive' is given.

Recently I heard that not all children grow out of hyperactivity. I asked Dr Herbert what he thought about this.

'There is a tendency to grow out of hyperactive behaviour,' he said. 'It has something to do with maturity. Motor incoordination and excess becomes more easily self-controlled as the child develops. However, as some children near their teens their conduct worsens while the motor excesses lessen. They may become more anti-social and some may become delinquent.' Was it possible that some adults were hyperactive, I asked?

'Yes,' he said. 'In some people hyperactivity can go on into adolescence and adulthood, but by then it is probably termed a conduct disorder.'

There seem to be various theories for the cause of

hyperactivity so I asked Dr Herbert what he felt were the reasons for it.

'There are many contributory causes. For example, there may be genetic factors involved. Hyperactivity is often found in children who are brain damaged in one way or another, so it could be associated with birth difficulties or medical problems arising during pregnancy. There is also the effect of lead poisoning or allergic reactions on the child. All these things can be influences, and there are other possibilities. Some children may be affected by their environment, such as a very neglectful, disturbed home.

'Of course,' he added, 'there are different types of behaviour and temperament evident in children from birth. Some are a delight to raise as they have very placid temperaments. Others are very temperamental. They tend to be resistant to training, biologically unpredictable, highly active and thus generally difficult children. They dislike changes in routine and are not malleable; such unhappy babies often grow into difficult children.'

Did Dr Herbert know of any link between mental illness later in life and hyperactivity in children?

'There is no causal link with serious psychiatric illnesses. The link is rather with antisocial problems. The hyperactive child is resistant to socialisation and this can predispose delinquency if not dealt with in childhood. Children learn to become problems by having faulty models of what is right – or they fail to learn to respect the standards and obligations of social life. Unless the appropriate "social" and "moral" lessons are learned during childhood – value judgements, self-control, respect for the other's point of view, and many other aspects of moral development – the hyperactive child is at risk of remaining an antisocial being, manifesting delinquent or other psychological disorders.'

I wondered if Dr Herbert used the label 'hyperactive' in dealing with certain children?

'Yes, if it is useful,' he agreed. 'Some parents find it helpful to have the child labelled "hyperactive". For instance, some mothers have been saying to themselves, "I am a failure as a mother." In that case it is helpful for them to realise that the child actually has a problem. They need to leave the label behind later and not use it as an excuse for inaction or pessimism. Some parents seem better equipped to cope with a hyperactive child. It depends on the parents and the child and how they respond to one another,' he added. 'Yes, I might label some children who are obviously so different – so long as the diagnostic term does not stop the child receiving help. And so long as it does not stop thought on how to teach the child to improve and does not mean that the parents believe that he *cannot* improve because he is hyperactive, then the term "hyperactive" may be useful.'

Having discussed these general ideas about the subject I felt eager to know Dr Herbert's ideas on helping the hyperactive child.

'The parents of a hyperactive child often say, "It is no use my telling him anything. He just doesn't listen,"' said Dr Herbert. 'I ask them to think of an example of when the child *has* taken notice of what they say. They can usually think of such times. How did they actually get a positive response from the child? Was it through a certain line of action they pursued? They have perhaps insisted that the child does not disturb them first thing in the morning and have repeatedly returned him to his bed to make the point clear. They have been really persistent *and* consistent! And he has learned.' (This rang a bell with me. That little early morning figure who whined pathetically, 'Mummy,' and tried to creep into bed, or wanted to get one or both of us out of bed to begin the day – yes, persistence worked at this point in my experience, although I felt guilty at being so unwelcoming to my child.)

'Perhaps it might work at other times and in other circumstances – if the same amount of conviction and pressure (particularly with mother and father insisting together) is put on the child to do what is required of him,' continued Dr Herbert.

'Parents sometimes think: he is hyperactive, or whatever the label may be, he cannot learn. We must put up with his behaviour. But he *can* learn! Parents need to analyse what the child is able to do and what he really cannot do. If they have conviction in their voice when they tell the child what to do or what not to do, he will respond. If they expect the child to be negative, he will be.'

Dr Herbert stressed to me that the psychologist does not have some magical formula and some mysterious way of dealing with children. It is purely common sense backed up by persistence, presented in a balanced form. He and his team of students teach parents the way to give a command effectively and to think about the words they are using.

How many times have you heard a mother say something like this to her child:

'Don't do that.'

The answer comes back:

'Why not?'

'Because I said no.'

The child may stop briefly and then start again.

'I said NO!' says mother.

'OH, MUM, PLEASE!'

'NO!'

Soon he comes back and takes up where he left off. By this time his mother is fed up with the whole thing and the child sees he is winning. Mum ignores what he is doing, or gives a weak reprimand to justify her original stand:

'Oh, didn't I say that you couldn't do that?'

Yes, I would agree with Dr Herbert. How easy it is to see the mistakes that occur when the confrontation is between someone else and their child, but I know from experience how hard it is to stand back and recognise what is happening between oneself and a child.

'The child who is hyperactive can learn to behave appropriately,' insists Dr Herbert, 'but the connection takes longer to make and more patience and persistence are needed.'

This statement reminded me of the difference between my son and my daughter. When he was about four-and-a-half years old we had to keep reminding John to eat rather than talk at the meal table. Each mealtime we found ourselves saying, 'John, be quiet. Eat.'

He would then take one mouthful and continue talking where he had left off. He needed a constant reminder to finish his food and meals became unhappy times for myself, my husband and no doubt John. Then one day we changed the plan. We did not remind him to eat at all. The first meal at which we tried this, he talked all through the first course. We finished eating and removed his untouched plate of food without comment. He looked surprised, but when I brought in the second course with none for him, he could not make out what was happening.

'I didn't think you were hungry today, John,' I said. At the next meal he sat at the table and ate his food quickly and quietly before it could disappear, and thereafter we had no further problems.

By changing our plan of action and sticking to it, we cured in one day a problem that had been with us for weeks. However in Tanya's case, when we made a plan of action to overcome a particular problem, we found that it took many months or years of persistence to bring about the desired change.

The difficulty that many parents face with a hyperactive child is which problem to deal with first, because there are so many. He may not be sleeping and continually comes down stairs. When awake he is causing havoc. He will not sit at the table at mealtimes. His brothers and sisters are having problems with his behaviour. Where does one begin?

Dr Herbert advises:

'In order to begin to cope with the child's problem it is necessary to get one's priorities right. What behaviour do we need to attend to first? The child so easily shapes the parent's behaviour rather than the parent shaping the child's. The mother (who is usually the parent who is in the forefront of this battle) has to regain confidence in her ability to cope with the child. Through the problems which she has experienced with her child, she may have developed hatred or resentment towards him. She may even have had fantasies of getting rid of the child. She is less confident and unsure of herself as a capable mother. It is helpful for the mother to have the support of another person at this time who can aid her in analysing the situation and reassure her, "Yes, that is the right thing to do."'

Dr Herbert pointed out what I had not previously considered, namely that the hyperactive child does not often see the consequences of his behaviour. He has moved on to the next thing so rapidly that he is not able to see what he has done.

'Parents should make the child aware of the result of his behaviour. If he is always stopped from what he is doing in order to prevent damage to himself, someone else, or inanimate objects, he will not learn that this action brings problems,' said Dr Herbert.

In Part One of this book I have described my own fears that following my child around trying to keep her out of danger and preventing too much destruction might have had an adverse effect upon her. Now Dr Herbert had given me a reason which I had not considered fully before. Of course, one still has to be careful, or the child's life could be in danger. Had I allowed my child to run into the road in order to teach her that it is a dangerous thing to do, there are several things she might have learned: cars knock people over and hurt them; cars screech to a halt and mummy gets told off by the driver; nothing happens which is different in the road (when the road is clear, of course); it may be too late to learn lessons for the future. The balance between learning lessons and ultimate safety is of course important, as Dr Herbert pointed out.

'Charts with stickers or colours are a good way of rewarding a child. He is allowed to stick on a star, or colour in a picture, when he has achieved a goal. It is something he can then show to the rest of the family for them to admire and he can see how well he has progressed. After receiving a certain number of points there is an added bonus for achievement. Of course,' added Dr Herbert, 'this also helps parents to look for good behaviour and not only notice the bad behaviour.'

I remember that this method helped my son, not with a behaviour problem but with learning to read. He doubted his own ability to learn, it seemed. The teacher he went to for extra help had a ladder on the wall with the names of all her pupils attached to numbered rungs. John never met the other children, but he worked very hard to see if he could move up the ladder week by week and overtake the others whom he knew only by name. He also knew that when he reached the top of the ladder he would have achieved success and would then be able to say 'goodbye' to his teacher and cope well in normal classes at school. In Tanya's experience we found that the reward of money for keeping her room tidy, rather than smacking her for making such an awful mess, proved highly successful.

Does physical punishment have a part to play in helping the hyperactive child? I asked Dr Herbert.

'The tolerance of pain in a hyperactive child is often high, so that they do not feel a slap,' he said. 'I would prefer "Time out", which is the removal of a child to another place where he can be left alone in safety for periods of up to five minutes, or a visual reward for good behaviour. Sometimes scolding the child works in reverse. We pay attention to the child when he is behaving badly and a slap can be a reward to the child as he then has his parents' undivided attention.

'A reward which is visible can help to show the child the cost of bad behaviour. For example, a jar of marbles or pennies. Bad behaviour removes a marble or penny, but there is a bonus scheme for keeping above a certain number of objects in the jar.

'When parents first begin to reward the child for good behaviour, they must sometimes begin at the point of rewarding behaviour that is better than the child's usual behaviour. Gradually the criteria for praise become higher as the child improves.

'It is very important to give attention to the child when he is behaving well. Often the parents are so relieved when the child is quiet that they enjoy the lull without remembering to reward the child for it.'

How true it is! I can remember how beautiful a few minutes' peace and quiet could be. Did I reward good behaviour? Not often enough, I am sure.

'Parents are often knocked off the track by other people who say that they cannot control their child', said Dr Herbert. 'They need reassurance – "You have a difficult child. Anyone would have similar problems with this child. We can teach you some techniques which will help you to cope." The parents set the example, they reward good behaviour and punish bad behaviour in a consistent way – this is what is termed "behaviour modification".

'When the parents are already tired and depressed the problem is greater and they find it more difficult to begin to modify the child's behaviour because they are at a low ebb. They need to reward themselves for the progress they have made in aiding their child. I would say to parents who have been using this method: "Reward yourselves every so often, as you make headway with your child. Give yourself a treat. Get a babysitter and go out for a meal together." It is important that the parents' morale is kept up when they are working with their child in overcoming a problem.'

Dr Herbert makes these statements, not from the comfort of his office, or as a theory expounded to his students. He is in the front line working with children who have problems and helping the parents or those caring for children, following through the plan of action that he advocates. He also trains his students to go into homes where children are causing concern and support the parents for a while in a programme of behaviour modification.

For example, a child has a sleep problem. When put to bed he constantly comes downstairs. A plan is laid so that the child will learn that this is not acceptable. Every time he comes down, he will be returned to bed and told firmly to stay there. He has to learn that however many times he comes down, the consequences will be the same – he will be returned to bed and the mother will not give up in despair. Initially this demands a great deal of courage of parents.

The routine is worked out first with the mother so that she knows in advance exactly what she is going to do and is therefore confident and in control. The child goes to bed, has a story and a cuddle and thereafter the mother must be firm and not accept defeat over the child's desire to come downstairs again and again. One of Dr Herbert's students sat up until two in the morning to help a mother persist in her decision to return her daughter to bed each time she came down. Persistence paid off and in the end the child accepted the routine. After the first night's struggle it was of course necessary to remain firm, but each evening the problem became less.

Dr Herbert uses behaviour modification with hyperactive children and with other children with behaviour problems, including handicapped children whose parents may have considered that their child is unable to learn. He cites the case of an autistic child whose mother had to sit in his bedroom until one o'clock each morning in order for him to sleep. If she tried to leave his room before that time he would immediately rouse from his shallow sleep and scream loudly. She had tried to ignore him, but he would then deliberately urinate over his bed. His mother then felt obliged to return to his room and change the bedclothes – and the problem began all over again. It was necessary to persuade the mother to allow the child to sleep in a wet bed in order to break him of the habit. His mother felt shocked at this idea and needed help to ignore the wet bed and his screams. The night that she tried leaving him to sleep in discomfort paid off, however. When she finally conquered the problem and saw her child respond, her joy turned to anger. 'Why didn't someone tell me about this before?' she asked.

Parents are not trained for the task that they must perform, Dr Herbert stressed. Many times as a mother I have wondered whether or not I am doing the best thing for my child. Am I being too kind and spoiling the child? Am I being firm, or am I being cruel? Am I helping my child, or am I injuring her view of other people for the rest of her life? Am I teaching my child or making life convenient for myself, showing her how to be selfish?

'What are the rules of the home?' asked Dr Herbert. 'Often these are not very explicit. They are unwritten laws which the parents may not be fully decided on and which are not well defined.'

I thought back in my marriage. Certain ways of behaving developed in our home; my husband brought in his ideas from his background and I brought mine. Between us we developed a code of conduct for our home which applied until we had our baby. As she grew up we modified these rules to include a child. As adults we saw what we were doing but did not necessarily discuss the reasons behind what we did with each other and we bent the rules to suit the occasion. Yet we expected our child to be aware of the rules and comply with them even when we ourselves were not very sure of what we were doing.

'Keep the rules of the household simple,' advised Dr Herbert. 'Which things are the most important? Work out the rules between husband and wife.'

This is very good advice on something that is often neglected. One cannot comply with rules about which one is unsure. Think of the variety of acceptable behaviour within some homes with which you are familiar. It is acceptable in one home for the children to use the furniture as play objects or rearrange the room to suit their play. Some parents unconcernedly allow the use of beds as trampolines. Others stipulate that toys must be put away in a specific place at a specific time, shoes must be removed and left in neat rows at the back door and slippers worn in the house. Beds must be turned back and left to air. Toothpaste should be squeezed from the bottom of the tube and the top replaced every time . . . and so on.

During our discussion it crossed my mind to ask how far parents should change to accommodate the child.

'The balance can go too far in favour of the child if parents are not careful. The child must adapt to parents and the parents to the child to a certain extent,' thought Dr Herbert.

One thing that worried me a great deal when my daughter was small was her apparent rejection of me. I tried to cuddle her and her lack of interest made it difficult for me to treat her with affection. Dr Herbert pointed out that there are children who are cuddlers and those who are non-cuddlers.

'Do not think that the child is rejecting you if he does not like being cuddled. So often the parents think that the child is rejecting them and in turn reject the child. It so easily becomes a downward spiral. Rejection of cuddling does not mean that the child is rejecting the parents. Everyone expresses himself in a different way.'

This may bring some comfort to parents facing a lack of response when they attempt to embrace their offspring. In my own case, my daughter now expects to be cuddled and seeks for this comfort, but years after I first tried to cuddle her. But how delightful it is!

Help in the management of a difficult child can be found by contacting the local Child Guidance Clinic. It is listed in the telephone book, usually under the name of the local county, under Educational Services. A telephone call will discover if a clinical psychologist is available to help parents with their child. Alternatively parents should ask their own doctor or the local Social Services Department about resources in their district.

14 Diet, Allergy and Pollution

TESTS FOR FOOD ALLERGIES
There are a number of standard tests used for food allergies at allergy clinics. The first step is to take a complete history of the patient's complaint and all the symptoms. Apparently unrelated physical and mental problems, when explained to another person, often make it appear that the patient is neurotic, so she may be cautious in describing how she actually feels. Some clinics recommend their patients to write down everything they eat over a period of days and the symptoms they experience. It is then sometimes possible to see a relationship between a certain food or foods and the symptoms, although the problem of 'masking' and 'addiction' may blur the pattern. One young woman had experienced severe cramp in the abdominal area. Her doctor gave her a thorough examination but could find no reason for it. He suggested that something in her diet might be causing her the problem. She listed all the foods she ate over a period of two weeks and noticed that cooking oil was the only item that she used every day. She left it out for a while and the cramps eased and disappeared. They reappeared when on holiday eating food cooked by other people. Not all food problems are as easy to solve, although this patient had suffered for a long time and might have continued to do so had the doctor not been alert to the possibility of food as the cause.

Some people have *fixed food allergies*. If they eat a certain food it always causes them problems. Others have *non-fixed allergies* which means that they are able to tolerate certain foods after they have left them out of their diet for a few days or longer, or if they eat them only occasionally and in small quantities. Other people have a mixture of fixed and non-fixed allergies.

One method of diagnosing food allergies is by means of *fasting*. By abstaining from food for a period of time it is possible to be certain that all the offending foods have been eliminated. Then the foods are individually reintroduced and the problems show up rapidly, as the symptoms are worse after a period of abstinence. The trial fast is usually for about a week. However if certain long term health problems are under investigation, such as asthma or eczema or ulcerative colitis, it is not always possible to maintain a fast for long enough for the person to have a remission in that time. In such cases a diet which excludes certain foods for periods of time is superior. A complete fast is not suitable for young children or for certain adults and should only be done under medical supervision.

When, by means of fasting or exclusion diets, it is suspected that a person is allergic to certain foods, *a pulse test* can be carried out after eating individual foods. The pulse is taken for a full minute before the food is eaten and again after eating at 20, 40 and 60 minutes. Symptoms which occur during the four hours after eating are also noted. A rise or fall in the pulse rate of 12 or more beats is considered to be significant. Sometimes it is found that the pulse rate does not in fact alter, yet significant symptoms occur. This is quite an effective method used by doctors to test foods.

A *rotary diversified diet* can be used to diagnose masked food allergies and is also useful as a way of treating and controlling problems for people who have multiple sensitivity. Foods of various kinds are eaten over a period of four or five days. Foods closely related, or the same foods, are not eaten on consecutive days. The person on the diet can then often identify the food which is causing problems. It is useful, too, as a treatment for some people, as after a while they are able to tolerate foods which previously affected them adversely. Help in planning a food rotation diet can be obtained from doctors who recommend its use or from the Allergy Analysis Service which is run by qualified alternative medical practitioners. The Service helps about 50 new patients a week who are recommended to them by a variety of people including doctors, health visitors, and alternative medical practitioners.

Advice is given on the telephone or by a personal visit. Mrs Simmonds, a qualified nurse, assists the patients with dietary difficulties and Mr Simmonds performs most of the tests they offer. They use 'dowsing' which is not a scientifically validated method, and their 'hair analysis' is not to be confused with the biochemically validated form of 'hair mineral analysis'. The latter is a measurement of the mineral content of the hair which is a reflection of the various processes occurring in the body and is useful for assessing calcium, magnesium, copper, zinc, chromium, selenium and the toxic metal status in the body. However, whatever one's views on that particular aspect of their work, they are very helpful in assisting people with diet. They recommend two books, *Food Allergy and the Allergic Patient* by Dr L. Taube, which explains the planning of a rotation diet, and *Chemical Victims* by Dr R. Mackarness. Both are available from Action Against Allergy (see addresses).

The *skin prick test* is not regarded as being very reliable in diagnosing allergies. People known to be allergic to certain foods show false reactions fairly frequently. This would mean that a child tested by this method might be advised to avoid a wide variety of food which is in fact not causing him any problem.

There is also another method which is not generally used by doctors, although it is becoming more popular with some medically trained people, as well as those using so-called 'fringe' methods. This is *muscle testing*, a series of tests used to identify foods or additives which cause problems for allergic or sensitive people. It is very simple to do and means that in a few hours tests can be made on the complete range of foods normally eaten by the patient. It is then possible to do spot checks at home after the initial problems have been identified. To me, a lay person, it seems to be extremely accurate, although I am told by a doctor that many people have been incorrectly advised on the basis of muscle testing and it is not a scientifically validated method. Before the tests are carried out a list of foods normally eaten by the patient is compiled and the individual foods are then tested one at a time by placing small quantities in the mouth. Different sets of muscles in the arms and legs are then tested for signs of weakness. The difference between the muscle response in most people is very obvious, when food which is good for them or is their allergen is tested. There is a method too for children or handicapped people who are unable to be tested in the normal way.

Muscle testing is based on applied kinesiology, the science of muscle testing, which is a much wider and more detailed study requiring years of training. It began being used by a chiropractor, George Goodheart, in 1964. John Thie researched the method and introduced it as a self help method for people in general. In Britain instructors are trained by Brian Butler of the British Touch for Health Association, and anyone interested in using this service should contact him or the Information Officer at the address given at the end of this book.

LEAD INTOXICATION
Throughout history there has been reference to lead pollution. As early as 20 BC it was considered that water stored in lead was not good to drink, yet 2,000 years later we are still only just beginning to be advised to remove lead water pipes from our homes. As a child, I remember my father replacing our lead water pipes. Prior to that we always ran the tap for a while before drinking from it. Apparently lead solder is still often used to join copper pipes. It is a fact that some children born apparently normal have, by the age of five, become severely subnormal through lead poisoning, prenatally via the mother (lead readily crosses the placenta) and/or postnatally, perhaps by chewing lead paint or through contamination from other sources.

Lead in the atmosphere comes mostly from lead additives in petrol, through emissions from factories and from scrapyards which are a problem in some areas. Fall-out from the air is a major source of lead in food crops exposed to free circulation of air, such as lettuce, spinach and broccoli, but not peas or cabbage heart. Thus most of the lead in our food started off in petrol tanks. Airborne lead is also absorbed directly through the lungs. The Clear Trust led a successful 'Get Lead Out Of Petrol' campaign. In 1983 the Government announced that it had agreed to the removal of lead from some (not all) petrol, possibly by 1990. However there are large numbers of children already affected by lead in their bodies and more will be affected until the lead additives are no longer used. At present, we seem to value our cars more than we do the health of our children (although leaded petrol has bad side effects on car engines, too).

Professor Bryce-Smith, Professor of Organic Chemistry at Reading University, is very concerned about lead pollution and its effects on children. He sees abundant evidence that hyperactivity is one of the symptoms of lead intoxication in children, even those who appear healthy by conventional criteria, but suggests that the poisonous effects of lead can be made worse by stress and poor diet. Rather than 'hyperactivity', he prefers to use the term 'hypoinhibition' which he feels is a more accurate term to use in describing the condition, as it is more to be associated with a lack of inhibitory control than the over-stimulation of excitatory functions in the brain.

In some cases, he feels, there is undoubtedly an association between food allergies and hyperactivity, and dietary control can prove helpful. It still leaves us with the question of what actually causes wholly unnatural hypersensitivity to certain items of food. Although the more fundamental causes are not yet well-understood, it is his personal belief that the answer is likely to be found in neurotoxic factors in our environment operating in combination with nutritional deficiencies of essential elements.

The levels of two essential nutrient elements, calcium and zinc, were measured in the bones of still-born infants. Many abnormally low levels of calcium were found and a few cases of very low zinc levels. Of the two anti-nutrients, cadmium and lead, in the bones of the babies, average levels of lead were five to ten times higher than those for apparently normal infants and the levels of cadmium were also similarly raised in 45 per cent of the stillbirths, giving evidence that lead from a mother's diet can harm the foetus.

Children of school age who are hyperactive are often behind in education compared with other children of their age. They appear to be bright but their behaviour causes problems to the teacher and distracts the other children, and their own progress is slowed down. Their actual ability shows up best in verbal rather than written tests, it seems, and they cannot produce the work that is expected of them. It is Professor

Bryce-Smith's view, supported by a considerable weight of evidence, that those hyperactive children not known to have organic brain damage, together with many children who have specific learning difficulties of the dyslexia type, and children who are mentally handicapped from no known cause, are affected by 'sub-clinical lead poisoning'.

Children and their parents now have bodily burdens of lead between 100 and 1000 times greater than the 'natural' levels in their pre-technology ancestors. This is as a result of high exposure from car exhaust and factory emissions and of much modern technology with its use of lead in paint, food cans, pottery glazes, and so on. However, it seems likely that between 50 and 80 per cent of our body lead comes from lead additives in petrol. This means that children who live in large cities are most at risk. Food grown close to the worst areas of lead pollution gathers the airborne fall-out, the outer leaves being typically contaminated ten times higher than the inner leaves. The dust in urban houses, streets and schools is sometimes so rich in lead that it could be worked as a lead ore. This dust finds its way onto children's fingers and toys, and young children are particularly vulnerable as they put their fingers into their mouths, as well as objects other than food. If it becomes compulsive to suck and chew non-food objects, the condition is called 'pica', and it is especially noticed if the child has an emotional disturbance or if calcium, zinc, iron, or all of these are deficient in his diet.

Even so-called 'normal' levels of lead in children now seem to be actively harmful. It is only recently that this has been recognised, probably because it is so common that the symptoms have come to be regarded as normal behaviour, and also because they do not appear in categories of illness which are within the medical ambit. These so-called subclinical symptoms include hyperactivity in some children and a general dulling of intelligence in others, according to Professor Bryce-Smith. Lead is a neurotoxin – in other words, a poison to the brain – as it affects the brain chemistry, and the child's brain is one of the main target organs. Children who show none of the conventional symptoms of clinical poisoning and no obvious signs of neurological damage can still have lead-induced mental dysfunction. It is a particularly nasty feature, feels the

Professor, as the children appear perfectly healthy. The symptoms are present, but they tend to appear, not in the surgery, but in the classroom and the juvenile court.

It used to be thought by many people that a child's brain is fully developed in the physical sense at the time of birth. It is now known that this is not so and that the development of the central nervous system continues after birth and maybe even up to around 18 years of age. At birth, the cerebellum is probably the least well developed region of the brain, and has only about seven per cent of the cells of the adult. In particular, the cerebellum controls fine movements. Anything which hinders the normal maturing of the brain can present problems, and lead certainly does that.

Each neuron in the brain has a large number of fine nerve fibres coming from other cells, which appear to attach themselves. Although they carry an electric current there is in fact a gap at the nerve ending which is called a synapse. This synapse is considered to be the decision-making area of the brain. Each neuron may have an average of 10,000 synapses, so each neuron should be linked to 10,000 others to form a network. Electrical impulses cannot pass across these synapses directly; when an impulse reaches the gap it causes the release of molecules called neurotransmitters into the gap. Over thirty neurotransmitters have so far been identified. These include acetylcholine, noradrenaline, or the histamine which plays a part in allergic reactions. They carry the impulse or 'message' across the gap to the adjoining cell membrane where they join on to receptor proteins, thereby opening 'gates' in the membrane. One type of gate is the right size to allow sodium ions to enter into the next cell. This movement of ions provides an excitatory message to the nerve cell and if it receives enough messages of this type from its many synapses, a new electrical impulse is discharged along its nerve fibre: the neuron 'fires', as it were, and the sodium ions pull the trigger. This happens over and over again in the process of relaying the original impulse onwards.

There are other cells with an inhibitory function which act to balance the excitatory function just described. They release a different neurotransmitter molecule which opens a smaller 'gate' into the adjoining cell, through which the sodium ion cannot pass. Instead the smaller potassium ions pass out from the cell into the synapse, in the opposite direction to that of the excitatory sodium ions. This contrary movement instructs the cell not to fire. (The effect is electrical in nature as both sodium and potassium ions carry a positive charge). The balance between the impulses received by a neuron from the various excitatory and inhibitory neurotransmitters determines whether the message is passed on or not – that is, whether the neuron 'fires'.

If for any reason the inhibitory functions are damaged more than the excitatory functions, the system tends to show excessive hair-trigger sensitivity to impulses. The person will tend to over-react to messages reaching him from his brain or environment. There will be an excessive level of restlessness typical of that of the hyperactive (or hypoinhibited) child if the motor nerves are affected. One of the main effects of lead at so-called 'low' levels in children is to impair selectively the inhibitory functions and thereby alter behavioural responses to induce hyperactivity. There is also an increased sensitivity to stress – social stress as well as certain types of dietary stress. Some children suffer a dulling of intellect by exposure to lead, and this may occur either with or instead of the behavioural disturbances.

In the case of children with high levels of lead in their bodies, Professor Bryce-Smith gives the following recommendations:

> The toxic effects of lead may be offset to a useful degree by a diet which is rich in calcium, phosphate and protein (not too rich, however) and low in fat. The diet should also be well supplied with other minerals such as magnesium and iron and a general multi-vitamin supplement is desirable, especially one containing zinc. Should the latter prove unobtainable, a dietary zinc supplement may be given providing five milligrams of Zn per day for a child and 15 mg for an adult. All canned food and all shellfish, liver and kidney, whether canned or not, should be avoided. Fruits rich in pectin, such as apples and bananas, are helpful, but above ground fruit and vegetables (except cabbage heart and peas) grown near traffic and in all the Greater London areas, are liable to be seriously lead contaminated, and should be

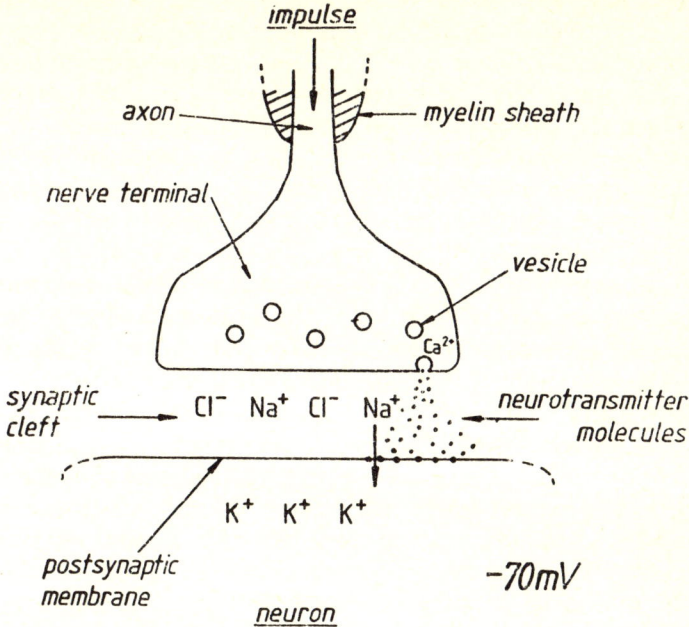

impulse

axon ———————— *myelin sheath*

nerve terminal

vesicle

Ca^{2+}

synaptic cleft ⟶ Cl^- Na^+ Cl^- Na^+ ⟵ *neurotransmitter molecules*

K^+ K^+ K^+

postsynaptic membrane

$-70mV$

neuron

Excitation – Na^+ enters neuron, –ve potential falls

Inhibition – Cl^- enters neuron, or K^+ leaves, –ve potential rises

Excitatory and inhibitory processes at the synapse

avoided. All fruit and vegetables should be thoroughly washed.

Do not use water from the hot water system for drinking or cooking and run the cold tap first thing in the morning to flush the pipes. If you live in a soft water area (where soap lathers very readily and gives little 'scum') and in a pre-war house or one known or suspected to have lead water pipes, drink bottled mineral water and use the purified water available from most chemist shops for cooking and making tea, etc. (Meanwhile get your local Water Authority or

Environmental Health Department to test the water. Lead levels above 20 micrograms per litre or 0.02 milligrams per litre indicate significant contamination).

Do not use glazed earthenware vessels for cooking (Pyrex or similar is excellent), or for storing beer, wine, or fruit juices. Alcohol is best avoided while symptoms persist.

If lead is a factor, some marked improvement should be noticeable fairly quickly. Once an improvement has become firmly established, some relaxation in the above diet and reduction in the dietary supplements may be initiated, provided that there is no tendency to slip back to the former condition. However, it would be as well to continue to abstain from canned food, organ meat, and shellfish.

For an adult, a daily supplement of calcium (Ca) and phosphorus (P) of 700 mg and 500 mg respectively has been shown to produce a drastic reduction in lead absorption. For a child these amounts should be halved. Bone meal tablets provide calcium and phosphorus but are not recommended as they also contain lead. Prolonged intake of any dietary supplement should only be continued if there is medical advice to this effect.

(Professor D. Bryce-Smith, from 'Lead Induced Disorders of Mentation in Children; *Nutrition and Health*, 1983, 1 (3/4), 179–193. More detailed information given in the report *Lead or Health* – see book list).

FOOD WATCH

This is a Technical Advisory Service run by Mr Peter Campbell BSc, FIFST and his wife. Mr Campbell has been in the food industry for many years, working first with dairy products, later with food colours and finally with frozen pastry and meat products. He gave up his last job as a technical manager to set up Food Watch full time. Mr and Mrs Campbell did this for very personal reasons. She had suffered ill health and had been unable to find lasting relief from doctors. Eventually they discovered that she had food intolerances and her health has now improved so much that she is able to work with her husband in this enterprise. In fact he was so impressed by the results when his wife changed her diet that he willingly gave up a secure and well paid position in order to tell other people and assist them in obtaining unadulterated food.

In a talk which he gave to a group of parents of hyperactive or allergic children, he discussed the amount of stress that people have in their lives. Everyone is encouraged to get the most out of life and as we try to reach fulfilment we cause ourselves to suffer from stress. In some parts of the world this is not known as the people lead a simple and stressless life. In one generation we have seen the introduction of radio, television, cars, aeroplanes and atomic bombs. Our bodily systems have been overstretched. During this generation the air which we breathe has become polluted by the things we have invented. Within our own homes we have gas fires and many people smoke, causing the air to be too contaminated to be safe to breathe.

Added to this there is our food. Many things are now permitted by law to be added to food, which have never been eaten by human beings before. They have been added without sufficient consideration as to what the long term effects might be. What happens is that people are intolerant of them and the weakest part of the body is affected first. Intolerances develop when the personal system cannot cope with what is being introduced into the body. Children often become hyperactive and adults show high levels of irritability. Mr Campbell feels that doctors could be saving a large proportion of their time, since many chronic conditions they now treat are a direct result of food problems. Even breast milk, which is far superior to bottle feeding, can be polluted. There have been reports of DDT being found in breast milk in some parts of the world. Mr Campbell recommends that we buy convenience foods as little as possible and that the list of ingredients should be studied carefully. However he points out that not everything which has been used in the processing of the food is mentioned on the tin or package. Also, there may be occasions when, for several reasons, the ingredients are not exactly as stated on the container.

In discussing bread and flour, Mr Campbell mentioned that wholemeal flour has no additives. Wheatmeal flour may be white flour with added bran and white flour is treated with chemicals (benzoyl peroxide and others). New regulations which will soon be in force could mean that additives will be permitted in wholemeal bread. At present wholemeal bread has less added to it than white and brown bread. The additives involved are ascorbic acid (vitamin C), I-cysteine hydrochloride and azodicarbonamide. Also it is proposed that bleaching agents, chlorine dioxide, chlorine and benzoyl peroxide will be permitted. The proposals have been made by the Ministry of Agriculture, Fisheries and Food. The present wheatmeal or wheatgerm bread will in future have to be called brown to avoid confusion with wholemeal bread. Theoretically, people will be able to see what is in the bread by reading the packaging or by asking the baker what it contains, although he will only know what he himself has added – perhaps not everything added to the flour before he bought it. The wholemeal flour sold in smaller packages to the public (1½ kilo bags) will stay additive free, so the best way to avoid problems is to bake one's own bread. Mr Campbell sees that these alterations will cause many problems in the future, but it does not seem possible to do anything to alter the decision. (Talk given in 1983.)

Food Watch supplies people who are, or have been, patients at allergy clinics in Britain with food to replace food that they have been told they cannot eat. He obtains specific food that will not cause problems to various groups of people with food intolerance problems. He gives talks to self help groups, too, and supplies the members with foods that they need. The prices are kept purposely as low as possible, as Mr Campbell wants to avoid people paying unnecessarily high prices just because they need a special diet. Here are some examples of the food supplied (there are over 70 at present):

Margarine (milk-free), stoneground wholemeal flour, untreated white bread flour, breakfast cereals made from rye, barley, oatmeal, millet, etc., brown rice, soya products, dried fruit (untreated with sulphur dioxide), nuts, sweeteners including raw cane sugar, date palm sugar and fructose, goat's milk and cheese, carob powder, egg white replacer, various spreads made from fruit with no added sugar, colour or preservatives, and so on.

Food Watch supply a list of the foods available with a price list, and parcels will be sent to customers in return for cash with the order. When visiting groups, Mr Campbell takes a selection of food with him for sale and delivers bulk orders to groups in certain areas of the country. The address for Food Watch is listed at the back of this book. Food Watch have also prepared a cookbook to help people use the food effectively, *The Food Watch Cook Book* by Honor Campbell. This is also available directly from Food Watch.

FORESIGHT

This association was formed to take all possible steps to see that every baby who is born is free from congenital deformity and mental damage and is in perfect health. Foresight is concerned that many thousands of babies have congenital anomalies and the figure for perinatal death is too high. If pre-conceptual care were given, Foresight believes that these numbers could be greatly reduced. The association is also concerned that babies born normal later succumb to allergic syndromes, hyperactivity, learning difficulties and other health problems. Much, they feel, can be done through education of prospective parents and improvement of their diet. Work done with animals has shown that diet has a direct effect on the life of the young. Animals fed on inadequate diets abort their young or give birth to deformed offspring. Foresight feels that if the parents have an adequate diet the health of the unborn child can likewise be improved and death prevented.

The disadvantage of modern convenience foods which may deplete the body of essential vitamins and trace minerals, so putting the foetus at risk, is pointed out by the association. One example is that of zinc deficiency. The consumption of alcohol, water from copper pipes in soft water areas, and the birth control pill, all combine to deplete the body of stores of zinc. Refined foods, the processes used to freeze foods, the use of artificial fertilisers and so on, reduce the amount of zinc which would be found in food in its natural form.

Forsight aims to set up clinics where parents can receive advice and have a thorough health check a few months prior to an intended pregnancy. These are private clinics and the addresses are available from the association. Potential health hazards such as nutritional deficiencies and heavy metal burdens in the body, such as lead, are detected. Allergies and malabsorption syndromes are dealt with and advice on necessary supplements to diet are given. Advice on the best nutrition, the dangers of drugs, smoking and alcohol during pregnancy is given and also advice on breast feeding.

The association supports relevant research and has also been collecting information from all its clinics for five years and analysing the data. It also intends to follow up subsequent pregnancies and the progress of the mother and child. Information booklets are available from Foresight including *Guidelines for future parents* and *Environmental factors and foetal health – the case for pre-conceptual care*, as well as a wholefood cookery book.

One person who would undoubtedly have been interested in the work of Foresight was Ellen G. White, a pioneer in the field of diet and health whose views are described in the following section.

DIET IN PREGNANCY AND CHILDHOOD
Towards the end of the last century, when Ellen G. White was writing on diet and health, views on the relationship between diet and health were still very confused; yet this enlightened author wrote positively about the relationship between food and physical and mental health and published many books on practical aspects of living. This is what she said about food during pregnancy:

> Many advisers urge that every wish of the mother should be gratified; that if she desires any article of food, however harmful, she should freely indulge her appetite. Such advice is false and mischievous. Two lives are depending upon her, and her wishes should be tenderly regarded, her needs supplied. But at this time above all others she should avoid, in diet and in every other line, whatever would lessen physical or mental strength. (*Ministry of Healing*, p 373.)

> Great changes are going on in her system. It requires a great amount of blood, and therefore an increase of food of the most nourishing quality to convert into blood. Unless she has an abundant supply of nutritious food, she cannot

retain her physical strength, and her offspring is robbed of vitality. (*Counsels on Diet and Foods*, p. 219.)

She goes on to discuss the feeding of children and how wrong diet can cause problems, including irritability and excitement:

Children who eat improperly are often feeble, pale, and dwarfed and are nervous, excitable, and irritable. (*Ibid*, p. 231.)

The greatest danger of the young is from a lack of self-control. Indulgent parents do not teach their children self-denial. The very food they place before them is such as to irritate the stomach. The excitement thus produced is communicated to the brain, and as a result the passions are aroused. It cannot be too often repeated, that whatever is taken into the stomach affects not only the body, but ultimately the mind as well. (*Ibid*, p. 243.)

Many do not seem to understand the relationship the mind sustains to the body. If the system is deranged by improper food, the brain and nerves are affected, and the passions are easily aroused. (*Ibid*, p. 241.)

I wonder what she would say about the diet that many of us eat today? We may be apparently well fed, but the type of food and the additives in it would, I should think, cause her to put pen to paper if she were alive to see what is happening.

She also described the importance of educating the appetite of children:

The importance of training children to right dietetic habits can hardly be overestimated. The little ones need to learn that they eat to live, not live to eat. The training should begin with the infant in its mother's arms. The child should be given food only at regular intervals, and less frequently as it grows older. It should not be given sweets, or the food of older persons, which it is unable to digest. Care and regularity in the feeding of infants will not only promote health, and thus tend to make them quiet and sweet-tempered, but will lay the foundations of habits and will be a blessing to them in after years . . . Often they are permitted to eat what they choose and when they choose, without reference to health . . . then comes sickness, which is usually followed by dosing with poisonous drugs. (*Ibid*, p. 230.)

While children should be taught to control the appetite, and to eat with reference to health, let it be made plain that they are denying themselves only that which would do them harm. (*Ibid*, p. 231.)

The writer advocated a simple, balanced diet with plenty of fresh vegetables, fruit and pure water, together with exercise, fresh air and adequate sleep. She recommended that preserved food should be kept in jars rather than tins. Many of the points that various people have mentioned in this book as being helpful to children who are hyperactive, she recommended nearly a century ago. As for the idea that unsuitable food affects the mind – this is still a matter of controversy – proved by some, to their satisfaction, and rejected by others who disregard food as having a relationship to the health of the mind.

15 Alternative Medicine

THE HERBALISTIC APPROACH
A number of parents of hyperactive children whom I
interviewed stated that they now visit medical herbalists with
their children. I visited a herbalist myself to see what are his
views on the subject.

Mr David Potterton, ND, MBNOA, MNIMH, is a
Consultant Medical Herbalist and a Registered Naturopath.
He is a member of the National Institute of Medical Herbalists
and of the British Naturopathic and Osteopathic Association
and also belongs to the Royal Society of Medicine and the
McCarrison Society, a medical organisation devoted to the
study of health and nutrition. In addition to his work as a
herbalist and naturopath, he is also a medical journalist and
writes on a wide variety of health, medical and paramedical
subjects, including his own specialised fields, but he uses only
herbal and non-toxic medicines in his practice. In this capacity
he was one of the first people in Britain to write about
nutritional hyperactivity following the publication of Dr Ben
Feingold's book, *Why Your Child is Hyperactive*, in 1974. He
corresponded with Dr Feingold and then wrote an article in the
general practitioners' journal *Doctor*.

Mr Potterton told me that there is no specific herbal
approach to hyperactivity. As far as he is concerned, he
determines initially whether the child is actually hyperactive or
whether it is the parents who cannot cope with a normal child.
He studies the child's case history carefully, with particular
reference to the birth, to see whether the child was born
naturally or whether there were complications such as a forceps
delivery. Then he considers whether the child's hyperactivity

has been acquired since birth and the possible reasons for this.

Mr Potterton is ready to admit that his views on Dr Feingold's theory on the treatment of hyperactive children have broadened over the years. He believes that artificial food colourings and preservatives are liable to cause hyperactivity in human beings because the body cannot cope with foreign substances. Some natural substances, for example nutmeg, may also cause hyperactivity. He is concerned that people should eat as natural a diet as possible. He feels that parents may go to great lengths to remove colourings and preservatives from the child's diet and yet the diet may not be adequate to supply the child's nutritional needs, while retaining certain junk foods which contain insufficient nutrients for obtaining really good health. Parents become frustrated, he finds, trying to avoid the various substances which may be causing the problems, when there may be additional physiological reasons, such as a sluggish liver, about which they know nothing. The child may become undernourished and neurotic as a result of continually tampering with his diet, particularly in the case of parents who have no close support from the Hyperactive Children's Support Group or a doctor who is in agreement with the line of approach and willing to assist.

A diet too high in calories may produce one of two things, points out Mr Potterton. Either the child becomes overweight or he becomes hyperactive. He examines the diet the child eats and adjusts it to contain only sufficient calories required for normal needs. He replaces artificial foods in the diet with whole natural foods and reduces the refined sugar intake, as sugar affects the liver making it unable to cope efficiently with allergies. He has found that if specific foods do cause restlessness they tend to be artificial foods. He may use elimination diets which exclude certain groups of foods for periods in order to isolate those substances which cause problems. There is a great deal of documentation on the subject of allergies and, theoretically, one can become allergic to anything. Heredity can have a part in allergy problems as certain people cannot completely metabolise certain substances in food. Some people also seem unable to excrete lead from their body and it becomes deposited in the brain where it causes problems, including hyperactivity.

'What the body really needs is fresh air, fresh water and pure food,' Mr Potterton says.

The diet he recommends is as follows:

Food should be left as close to its natural state as possible. Stored, canned and packeted or precooked food should, whenever possible, be replaced by fresh food. The protective value of a wide range of fresh vegetables, fruits and dairy produce is particularly important. Breast feeding should always be encouraged. Cereal carbohydrates should not be refined. Sugar consumption should be at the absolute minimum.

Hyperactivity in the USA has been over-diagnosed and over-treated, he says, often on the basis of the child's behaviour in the classroom (which, he points out, is an unnatural environment anyway). In Britain hyperactivity is underdiagnosed. Herbalists are against the use of strong tranquillising drugs as a first choice therapy for hyperactivity. They see medication only as a way to help people to recover, not as an end in itself. Herbal medicines act as a tonic to the internal organs and aid digestion and absorption, helping to eliminate irritating substances. Food in general may have a relaxing or a stimulating effect on the body depending on what it is. Herbal medicine is used to relax the system and to assist the absorption of food, using only the amounts required to obtain the desired results.

I asked Mr Potterton how parents wanting to contact a herbalist may find a consultant. He suggests that they look in the Yellow Pages of the Telephone Directory and choose a qualified herbalist, one with the letters MNIMH or FNIMN after his name. The training for Naturopathy is a four year full-time course, as is the training for Herbalism. If the parents have difficulty in finding a herbalist they could write to the Secretary of the National Institute of Medical Herbalists, 41 Haverly Road, Winchester.

OSTEOPATHY
The founder of osteopathy, Andrew Taylor Still, believed that there is a very deep relationship between the structure of the body and the way in which it functions. He developed his ideas

over one hundred years ago and in 1971 The Society of Osteopaths was founded to promote the highest academic and practitioner standards in osteopathy. Members of the Society are graduates from osteopathic schools which provide at least four years full-time tuition in osteopathy. As in the United Kingdom osteopathy is practised under Common Law, membership of the Society assures the public that all the Society members are able to practise with safety and skill and are knowledgeable in medicine and osteopathy. Osteopathic treatment aims to balance the spine and its tensions and regulate the body systems as a whole. The spine is not, however, considered to be the only cause of problems. It recognises other causes of illness or disease, such as dietetic, psychological, developmental and bacteriological, to be important. The body is viewed as a series of inter-related and interdependent functions which in illness can affect each other, leading to chronic illness.

In the 1930s osteopathic treatment of the cranium began. At that time it was discovered that the fluctuation in pressure of the cerebro spinal fluid could be felt both in the head and sacrum. This fluid bathes the whole of the brain and spinal cord for the purpose of nutrition and protection. Rather than the skull being a solid box, it has been found that it is capable of movement along the joints between the bones. The whole skull is able to expand and contract in response to fluctuations of cerebral spinal fluid around the brain and spinal cord. Sometimes it is found that there is a restriction of movement of the bones of the cranium so that this expansion and contraction does not occur correctly. The reasons for this are many, but injury at birth, through forceps delivery or long labour, for example, are common. This lack of correct movement can affect different parts of the body, causing all kinds of symptoms such as headaches, learning disability, behavioural problems or other medical disorders. A recent textbook on the subject is *Craniosacral Therapy* by John E. Upledger and Jon D. Vredevoogd (published by Eastland Press, Chicago). They have a section on behavioural and learning disorders and have found relief for hyperactive children through correction of compression of the occipital condyles. The correction is very gentle and the child often falls asleep soon after the correction has been made, whilst still being treated. One treatment does not always give permanent relief, but four treatments are the most that have ever been needed to deal with recurrence of the compression. The authors have found that hyperactive children's behaviour alters dramatically following treatment and hyperactivity does not recur once the correction has been successful.

The authors note that some hyperactive children respond well to other approaches, such as an alteration in their diet; they do not claim that the cause of all hyperactivity is craniosacral system dysfunction. On the other hand, the craniosacral system has far reaching effects on other parts of the body, for example, the vagus nerve and the pituitary gland. They feel that this may therefore be an underlying cause of food intolerances, hypoglycemia episodes and so on. They see that there is a relationship between hyperactivity and condylar compression of the occiput. They have also found that the treatment can have a beneficial effect on children who suffer from abnormal fears, although this is less frequently effective than for hyperactivity, and on those who have learning problems. About half of the children treated have shown improvements. One boy told how he could read whole words after treatment, whereas previously he only saw words in small pieces of two or four letters and was therefore slow when reading.

Since my daughter ceased to be hyperactive she has received osteopathic treatment. I cannot therefore say that it did anything to relieve that problem but I felt very surprised by other results. During the treatment, which is very gentle, she usually fell asleep. The osteopath treating her had had extremely overactive children fall asleep also, even though they normally never sleep in the day and have difficulty in sleeping at night. I did not look for any improvement after the first treatment, yet during the week that followed I suddenly noticed that Tanya's handwriting had grown larger and therefore more legible. It had been so minute that the teachers constantly complained they could not read it. She had resisted all attempts to persuade her to make larger letters. Also that week, she woke earlier and brighter in the mornings, getting up on time without needing to be called repeatedly. She came downstairs and said that she wanted a big breakfast before going to school, quite the reversal of her normal attitude. The corrections made by the osteopath remained stable after a few treatments. She did not want to attend the final treatment as she said that she felt no new benefit from the previous one and saw it as a waste of time. The final treatment showed she was right, and that in fact she did not need further help.

Osteopaths recommend that the treatment should be given as early as possible after birth or following an injury, to prevent problems occurring. A group of British osteopaths belonging to the Society of Osteopaths have been trained to do treatments for hyperactive children, but not all osteopaths practise these techniques. If parents want help for their child they can obtain a list of Registered Osteopaths from the General Council and Register of Osteopaths (see addresses). They can also look in the Yellow Pages of the Telephone Directory to find an osteopath. A registered osteopath will have the letters DO, MRO after his name. They should ask the osteopath if he does cranial osteopathy, but one osteopath told me that, in his experience, normal osteopathic therapy treatment applied to the upper cervicals also helps to modify hyperactivity and encourage relaxation.

16 The Hyperactive Child as an Adult

Prior to writing this book I thought that hyperactivity persisted only in childhood and that children grew out of it as they matured. It may be that someone told me this when my daughter was younger. When, by her tenth birthday, the symptoms still persisted, I began to be concerned lest they continue and later combine with teenage troubles. To my relief she improved during the months which followed and we have now experienced two years of excellent behaviour with the revelation of a delightful personality.

Following my own experience, I subsequently met other parents whose children have not grown out of the symptoms associated with hyperactivity, but they have altered slightly and if anything become worse in certain respects. Since then I have found that a number of people have researched this aspect (mainly it seems in America) and some doctors in Britain are treating adults with problems related to hyperactivity. One American doctor became interested in the subject when parents told him of the problems they experienced with their dyslexic children. He realised that many of the parents had similar complaints themselves. He also noticed that some schizophrenics failed to respond to treatment and had similar characteristics to those suffering from 'minimal brain dysfunction' (this term is less used and the condition is usually described as 'hyperactivity', although this too is not an apt description to sum up the total behaviour).

Studies have been made revealing that, in some people, the hyperactive symptoms of childhood modify during the teens and adult life. Such adults go through life experiencing difficulty with relationships, over-reacting to situations and being easily distracted from the matter in hand, to mention just a few problems. Research has been carried out with the parents of hyperactive children, who were themselves considered hyperactive as children. A high percentage of them had become alcoholics and the others had problems including depression, obsessions, compulsive behaviour and undiagnosed mental illness. Studies have also been made of the siblings of hyperactive children, of hyperactive children as teenagers, of sustained attention and impulse control in hyperactive and normal children, and of the diagnosis of 'minimal brain dysfunction' in adults and its treatment.

It therefore seems wise to find out as soon as possible what is causing a child to be hyperactive, rather than hoping it will go away or masking it by the use of drugs. In at least some people it seems as if it can cause great problems later in life.

In the light of this, I am interested to hear that a group of people have set up a centre for teenage offenders who are so disturbed that the chances of their ever living a normal life are very slim. They are looking at every aspect of these young people rather than merely confining them to prevent their doing worse harm to other people. They give them complete health checks including tests to ascertain the level of lead or other toxic metals in their bodies, and test them for food allergies and sensitivities as well as dealing with their psychological, educational and emotional problems. In this way they hope to remove all the unseen causes of their problems so that they are not fighting an uphill battle which it is impossible to win, should there be underlying or contributory causes.

And in Conclusion . . .

Researching and writing this book has been an extremely interesting experience which brought me into contact with many people either affected by hyperactivity in their family or working to help those who are experiencing difficulties. There is a growing awareness of the problem – and a growing problem – in Britain. It is still difficult to obtain help from doctors. It seems as if the over-diagnosis of children in America and the immediate use of drugs for any child who shows symptoms has produced an over-cautious response outside the United States. Those who do treat hyperactive children successfully are much in demand, as are doctors who recognise its manifestations in adult life and seek to alleviate the symptoms rather than put them down to neurosis, marital difficulties or some other cause. The open-minded work of the Hyperactive Children's Support Group has done much to help distressed children and their distraught parents to obtain the aid of medical personnel and to link up research into various aspects, as well as to remove or reduce the problem in homes across the land.

By writing about my daughter's and other people's problems I had the intention of possibly helping others to find aid. However, one person has already benefited as a direct result of my work, prior to the publication of the book. That person is my own husband. It has brought great joy to me to find the answer to longstanding problems which have dogged his progress for many years. As a child he was very active and sometimes destructive (for example, he deliberately broke a desk at school despite warnings to leave it alone, and on one occasion was sent home by the teacher). He found school boring and had difficulty with the work. As a teenager he concentrated on music studies, since the practical work his father tried to teach him – such as mending a fuse or a puncture, painting and decorating or gardening – seemed difficult to comprehend and he had no patience to stick at a job for long. In his late teens he began taking on more and more activities, studying German and music more seriously and cycling miles a day to sell books for a publishing firm in order to earn the fees to attend a private college. He also found it well nigh impossible to relax. As a result he suffered a nervous breakdown from which he took years fully to recover. When I married him I saw him as a highly-strung person with an artistic temperament.

As the years went by various difficulties emerged. He showed sensitivity to sound, but often spoke very loudly and said that I could not hear him. Moderately bright light irritated him and made him screw his face up, giving him a strained appearance at times. He prided himself on not having a bad temper and being of even temperament, but he demonstrated tremendous swings of mood, from depression to unstable elation, which he refused to acknowledge as fact. He had a very poor image of himself and forever strove to become better qualified in order to be recognised as a useful person, when in fact he had many qualifications and abilities and did far more interesting things than the majority of people – for example, he has diplomas in public speaking, horticulture and remedial massage, and he teaches music.

Marital problems grew as a result of his swings of mood and he blamed me more and more for causing the problems, even at times when it seemed obvious to others that he had caused them. He also found decision-making difficult, yet often acted on sudden impulse, causing difficulties to arise later. Gastric trouble, which he had had intermittently since his teens, grew worse and made it more and more difficult for him to get to work in the mornings.

Over the years he had received little medical help of lasting value. It had ranged from a brief trial of some drugs to help him to relax, which made him too sleepy to work (but certainly made him relax!), a low residue diet at times when the gastric problem grew worse, and diagnosis of the trouble as irritation of the colon, possibly due to stress. The doctor suggested more than once that my husband should divorce me in order to remove the stress that I put on him. At one point I visited a psychiatrist at my husband's suggestion, as he felt that I needed help. The psychiatrist told me that I showed no signs of mental trouble, but suggested that my husband seemed neurotic and that I was getting and would continue to get a lot of emotional blackmail from him.

Then, suddenly, through reading, meeting people and taking down case histories for this book, it all fell into place. Could it be that my husband was a hyperactive adult? If so, could food be causing him his many difficulties? As the gastric trouble distressed him so much, he willingly agreed to investigate the possibility of allergies and food sensitivity. Tests on a wide range of his regular foods through muscle testing, revealed that his body is sensitive to colourings added to food during processing and to salicylates in certain foods. The following foods showed up as the cause of the trouble: cheese (a favourite food), ice cream (rarely eaten), skimmed milk powder (the brand we used for emergencies had added colour), orange squash (he had learned to avoid it as he always felt very ill if he drank any), margarine (we replaced it with a margarine from the health food shop without added colour) and another favourite – bananas. Two types of tinned nutmeats we used from the health food shop also contain artificial colour, which shows that the tins and packages must be read carefully wherever one shops. Since he has given up all these foods we have also found that tinned sweetcorn, fresh red and green peppers and petrol fumes also affect him. So it transpires that he is a good example of at least part of Dr Ben Feingold's hypothesis.

The result of his change in diet has been amazing. Within a week (during which time he felt extremely tired and appeared to have the 'flu) his body relaxed, he ceased to want to be doing something all the time, his mind became clearer and he began to feel better in health. The improvement has continued with a couple of setbacks when he accidentally took food with hidden colouring or skimmed milk powder as an ingredient. On one occasion his temperament changed immediately after he ate. An argument developed and he stormed out of the house and stayed away for hours, until mid afternoon, when we began to sort things out. His health problem has improved greatly, although he still occasionally gets pain in the colon; after years of trouble it is not possible for it to heal at once. He also finds that any food containing artificial colour gives him pain later and a stomach upset the following day. His general improvement has been so great that when he took a week's holiday he stayed at home relaxing, rather than trying to travel hither and thither and becoming frustrated and tired as usual.

At first he said that the improvement was because of me. He thought that I had changed and had ceased purposely to annoy him. Soon he began to see that *he* had changed and now says that he never wants to go back to his former troubles.

'I did not know that there was anything wrong with me. I thought that I was just being firm and expressing myself clearly,' he says.

We are now enjoying a second honeymoon after 15 years of marriage and delighting in each other's company more than we ever thought possible. We are happier than we have ever been. He is loving, kind, and thoughtful to me and the tension formerly in his body has drained away completely.

Finding the answer to this problem has revolutionised our family life and brought tremendous happiness to me, peace to our home and a relaxed atmosphere in which our children can grow up. I began by looking at theoretical answers to the problem of hyperactivity. My husband's experience has proved at least one theory to be true. I can confidently say, along with many of the parents I interviewed, 'I know it works.' I have a new husband and a happy marriage, but without having been near a divorce court. It is my hope that others with the problem of hyperactivity will reach as successful a conclusion as has my family.

Book List

Why Your Child is Hyperactive, Ben Feingold, MD, Random House Press, 1974.

Help for the Hyperactive Child, Sydney Walker III, MD, Houghton Mifflin Company, 1977.

The Myth of the Hyperactive Child and other means of child control, Peter Schrag and Diane Divoky, Penguin Books Ltd., 1981.

Psychiatric Aspects of Minimal Brain Dysfunction in Adults, Ed. Leopold Bellek, MD, Grune and Stratton, distributed in UK by Academic Press.

Allergies and the Hyperactive Child, Doris J. Rapp, MA, Cornerstone Library, 1979.

How to Control your Allergies, Robert Forman, PhD, Larchmont Books, 1979.

The Allergy Problem, Vicky Rippere, MA, BSc, MPhil, Thorsons Publishers, 1983.

Allergies your hidden enemy, Theron G. Randolf MD, Turnstone Press Ltd., 1980.

Not all in the Mind, Richard Mackarness, MB, BS, DPM, Pan Books.

Chemical Victims, Richard Mackarness MB, BS, DPM, Pan Books.

Nutrition and Health, Sir Robert McCarrison, from Wholefood, London.

The Strong-Willed Child, James C. Dobson, Tyndale House Publishers, 1978.

Helping Troubled Children, Dr Michael Rutter, Penguin, 1975.

Problems of Childhood, a complete guide for all concerned, Dr Martin Herbert, Pan Books, 1975.

Super Tactics for Super Parents, Kevin Wheldall, PO Box 363, Birmingham B15 2TT.

Behaviour can Change, E.V.S. Westmacott & R. J. Cameron, Globe Educational Books, through Macmillans, 1979.

Helping Clumsy Children, Ed. Neil Gordon & Ian McKinlay, Churchill Livingstone, Longman Group Ltd., 1980.

Behaviour Therapy with Hyperactive and Learning Disabled Children, Benjamin B. Lahey, Oxford University Press, 1979.

Lead or Health, Professor Bryce-Smith & Dr R. Stephens, from the Conservation Society.

Guidelines for Future Parents, booklet from Foresight.

Environmental Factors and Foetal Health – the case for preconceptual care, J. W. T. Dickerson, S. Baker & B. Barnes, booklet from Foresight.

The Foresight Wholefood Cookbook, Norman & Ruth Jervis, Roberts Publications, or from Foresight, 1984.

What Can I Give Him Today? (50 milk, egg and additive free recipes), Diana Wells, available from 32 Laburnum Ave., Kenilworth, Warwickshire, CV8 2DR.

The Food Watch Alternative Cookbook, Honor Campbell, available from Food Watch.

Useful Addresses

The Hyperactive Children's Support Group, Secretary, Sally Bunday, 59 Meadowside, Angmering, Littlehampton, West Sussex, BN16 4BW.

Wholefood Books, 24 Paddington Street, London W1M 4DR. Tel. 01-935 3924. *Books on Nutrition and Health, Malnutrition and Disease. Book list available.*

The Conservation Society, 68 Dora Road, London SW19.

Foresight, The Secretary, Woodhurst, Hydestile, Godalming, Surrey, GU8 4AY.

Society for Environmental Therapy, Secretary, 31 Sarah Street, Darwen, Lancs., BB3 3ET. *SET Newsletter, conferences for health professionals and lay members.*

National Society for Research into Allergy, Secretary, P.O. Box 45, Hinckley, Leicestershire, LE10 1JY.

Action Against Allergy, Amelia Nathan Hill, 43 The Downs, London, SW20 8HG. Tel. 01-947 5082.

Society of Osteopaths, Secretary, Simon Fielding, DO, MRO, 5 Bedford Place, Maidstone, Kent, ME16 8JB.

The General Council and Register of Osteopaths, 1–4 Suffolk St., London, SW1Y 4HG.

British Touch for Health Association (Muscle Testing), Brian Butler, 39 Browns Rd., Surbiton, Surrey, KT5 8ST. Tel. 01-399 3215. *or* Information Officer, Charles Benham, 29 Bushey Close, High Wycombe, Bucks., *or* Jane Thurnell-Read, 39 Turnpike Road, Connor Downs, Nr Hayle, Cornwall.

Food Watch, Mr Peter Campbell, High Acre, East Stour, Gillingham, Dorset SP8 5JR. Tel. 0747 85 261.

National Institute of Medical Herbalists, Secretary, 41 Haverly Road, Winchester.

British Naturopathic and Osteopathic Association, 6 Nether-hall Gardens, London, NW3 5RR.

Vegan Society, 47 Highlands Rd., Leatherhead, Surrey.

Allergy Analysis Service, 20 Taunton Road, Pedwell, Bridgewater, Somerset, TA7 9BG.

Inter-forum, 2 Park Street, Cirencester, Gloucestershire, GL7 2BN, Tel. 0285 68555.

Basingstoke Children's Helpline – for allergies and hyperactivity. Tel. Tadley 6662 *or* Kingsclere 298599.